GW00976126

Microsoft® Word®
Essentials
The Step-By-Step Guide

C.J. Benton

ISBN-10: 1544677863
ISBN-13: 978-1544677866

Thank you!

Thank you for purchasing and reading this book! **Your feedback is valued and appreciated**. Please take a few minutes and leave a review.

Other Books Available From This Author:

---

1. Microsoft® Excel® Start Here The Beginners Guide

2. The Step-By-Step Guide To The **25 Most Common** Microsoft® Excel® Formulas & Features

3. The Step-By-Step Guide To **Pivot Tables &** Introduction To **Dashboards** *(version 2013)*

4. **Excel® Pivot Tables & Introduction To Dashboards** The Step-By-Step Guide *(version 2016)*

5. The Step-By-Step Guide To The **VLOOKUP** formula in Microsoft® Excel®

6. The Microsoft® Excel® Step-By-Step Training Guide **Book Bundle**

7. **Excel® Macros & VBA For Business Users** - A Beginners Guide

Table of Contents

CHAPTER 1

An Introduction To Microsoft® Word®

Microsoft® Word® is a word processing application that provides users with the tools to create professional looking documents. Word® also contains the widely used feature called **Mail Merge** which allows you to create mass communications where specific sections can be tailored to individuals or groups.

Word® provides powerful editing and reviewing capabilities that help to minimize spelling mistakes and grammatical errors. These utilities also include the ability track and compare document changes made by other users. You may also extend Word's® functionality by creating predefined input user forms and macros to automate routine tasks.

Microsoft® Word® is part of the Microsoft® Office® suite. You may purchase Word® by itself or as part of the Microsoft® Office® collection. Depending on the package you buy, the suite typically includes four to seven of the below *desktop* applications:

1. **Access®** *(a database application)*
2. **Excel®** *(a spreadsheet application)*
3. **OneNote®** *(program stores text, web links, images and other information in one place)*
4. **Outlook®** *(an email application)*
5. **PowerPoint®** *(a presentation / slideshow program)*
6. **Publisher®** *(a tool to create professional looking flyers, advertisements, brochures, invitations etc.)*
7. **Word®** *(a word processing application)*

These applications are also available *online* via a subscription service called Office 365.

The four most widely used applications of the suite are, **Excel®, Word®**, **Outlook®**, & **PowerPoint®**. According to Microsoft®, there are more than 1.2 billion[1] users of Microsoft® Office®, making it the mostly widely used office software program in the world.

Basic knowledge and experience with Word® along with Excel® and Outlook® are essential skills for many professions and college students.

The following pages will introduce you to the basic functionality of Word®. You'll learn how to employ the most commonly used toolbar commands, such as how to create a new Word® document, formatting, saving, and printing. In addition to this, you'll gain experience applying Word's® practical features such as creating a Table Of Contents, inserting Watermarks, Tables (grids), SmartArt, using Spellcheck, the Thesaurus, and how to Track Changes. Concluding with a step-by-step review of the very beneficial Mail Merge utility.

When completed, you'll have a solid understanding of Word® and be ready to take the next step in your education of the Microsoft® Office® suite.

How To Use This Book

All of the examples in this book use Microsoft® Word® 2013, however, most of the functions can be applied with Microsoft® Word® version 2007 or later.

Please always **back-up your work** and **save often**. A good best practice when attempting any new functionality is to **create a copy of the original word document** and implement your changes on the

[1] *Data from Microsoft® by the numbers, retrieved 27 January 2017* http://news.microsoft.com/bythenumbers/planet-office

copied document. Should anything go wrong, you then have the original file to fall back on.

Diagram 1:

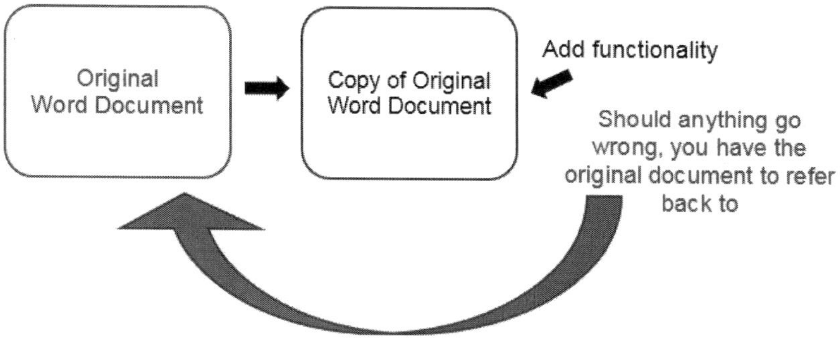

The table below is a summary of the features detailed in each section:

PART 1 – TEXT & PARAGRAPH FORMATTING	
Chapters 3 - 6	▪ **Bold,** *Italic,* Underline, ~~strikethrough~~ ▪ Font Styles and Sizes ▪ Text Highlighting ▪ Bulleted or Numbered lists ▪ Copy, Cut, Paste, & Format Painter ▪ Printing & Creating PDF Documents ▪ Paragraph Indentation & Line Spacing
PART 2 – PRESENTATION & GRAPHICS	
Chapters 7 – 13	▪ Page Breaks, Headers, Footers, & Page Numbers ▪ Tables & Table Formatting ▪ Page Orientation & Size ▪ Shapes, SmartArt, & Screenshots ▪ Table of Contents ▪ Document Formatting & Page Boarders
PART 3 – DOCUMENT REVIEW & EDITING	
Chapters 14 - 18	▪ Spellcheck & Thesaurus ▪ Find, Replace, & Go-To ▪ Track Changes & Document Compare ▪ Watermarks ▪ Read-Only & Password Protected Documents
PART 4 – MAIL MERGE	
Chapters 19 - 21	▪ Mail Merge – Form Letters ▪ Mail Merge – Mailing Labels

CHAPTER 2

Getting Started With Microsoft® Word® & The Toolbar (Ribbon)

To open Microsoft® Word®:

1. Click the *'W'* icon  on the **'Start Task Bar'**

or

2. From the **'Start'** menu, select '**All Programs'**
    a. Open the folder '**Microsoft® Office® *2013****'
    b. Click the program **'Word® *2013****'

**Depending on the version of Microsoft® Word® you have, the year may be 2016, 2013, 2010, or 2007*

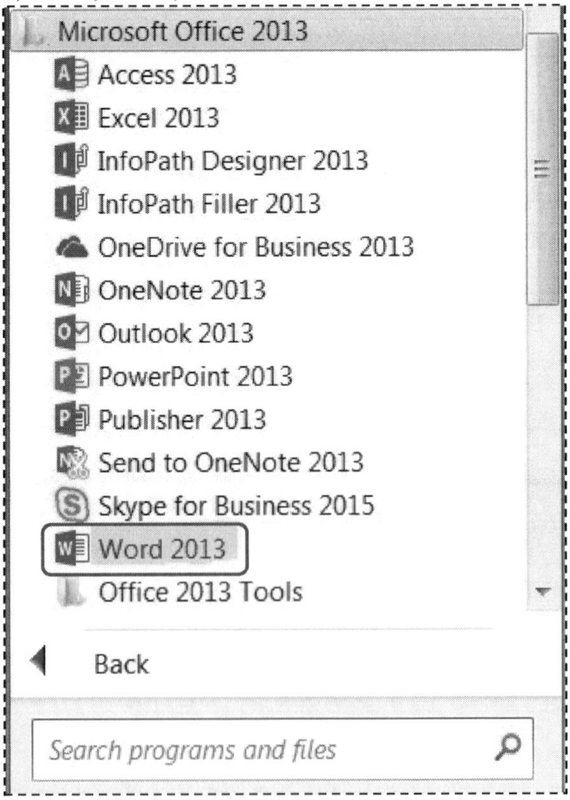

Once Word® has opened, your screen will look *similar* to the following. You'll notice pre-made templates available for download and a dialogue box to search for more pre-made files. The best practice is to learn the basic functionality of Microsoft® Word® before using these. Once you have a better understanding of how to navigate Word®, you can modify the settings in these templates to meet your requirements.

3. Select the **'Blank document'** option.

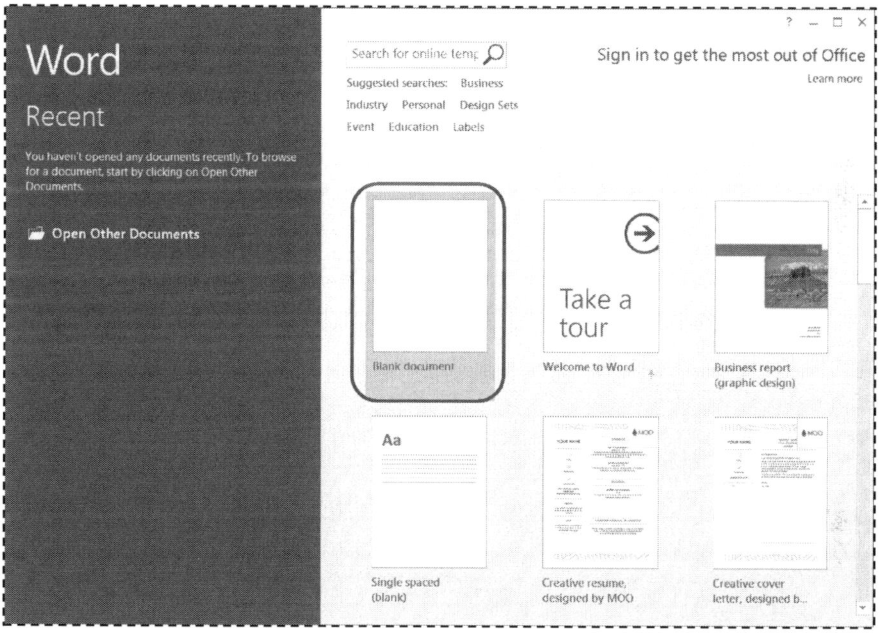

Ribbon (Toolbar)

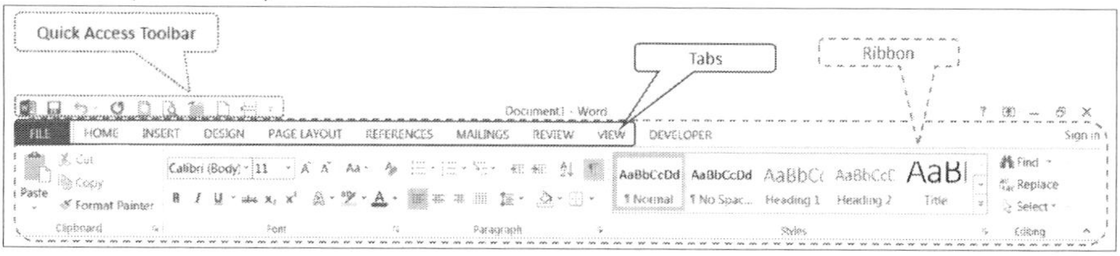

Let's take a closer at the **toolbar** or what Microsoft® calls the **'Ribbon'.** The **Ribbon** consists of tabs that contain application commands. There are nine default tabs.

1) File*
2) Home
3) Insert
4) Design
5) Page Layout
6) References
7) Mailings
8) Review
9) View

***Note**: the tab **'File'** does not contain commands, instead it provides information about the document, as well as options for **saving**, **printing**, and **exporting** the document file.*

Tab Description

HOME

The **'HOME'** tab contains commands for copying, cutting, pasting and formatting data. Including **Bold**, Underline, *Italic*, & ~~Strikethrough~~, **font types**, sizing, bulleted, and numbered lists.

INSERT

The **'INSERT'** tab contains commands for inserting page breaks, tables, headers, footers, and page numbers. Including presentation tools such as pictures, screenshots, and SmartArt

DESIGN

From the **'DESIGN'** tab you can apply pre-defined formatting to the *entire document*. Add a Watermark, apply a page border, or change the page color.

PAGE LAYOUT

The **'PAGE LAYOUT'** tab is where you can change the page orientation and size. Adjust margins and line spacing for paragraphs.

REFERENCES

From the **'REFERENCES'** tab you may insert a Table Contents, Index, add Footnotes, and include Citations.

MAILINGS

The **'MAILINGS'** tab is where you setup, test, and merge the form letters, labels, invoices, envelopes, emails tailored for each individual or organization.

REVIEW

Think of the **'REVIEW'** tab as your toolbox. In this tab, you'll find tools for checking Spelling, Grammar, a Thesaurus, a utility to translate text from another language, and the ability to Track Changes and compare or combine documents.

VIEW

From the **'VIEW'** tab you can control how Word® is displayed on your screen. You may choose different layout options such as Print, Read or Web, whether you see the Navigation Pane *(when utilizing style headings)*, the ruler, and can select different zoom *(screen size display)* choices.

Quick Access Toolbar

The Quick Access Toolbar sets on top of the Ribbon. This is where to add buttons that you use the most often. Functions such as save, print, undo, or creating a new document. These commands stay constant, regardless of what Ribbon tab is active.

Both the **Quick Access Toolbar** and the **Ribbon** are customizable. I find it more efficient to modify the Quick Access Toolbar. However, you may prefer to change the Ribbon.

Below are the steps to remove or add buttons to both the **Quick Access Toolbar** and **Ribbon:**

1. Click the **'File'** tab
2. Select '**Options'**
3. Select either **'Quick Access Toolbar'** or **'Customize Ribbon'**
4. Add or Remove the buttons you wish
5. Click the **'OK'** button

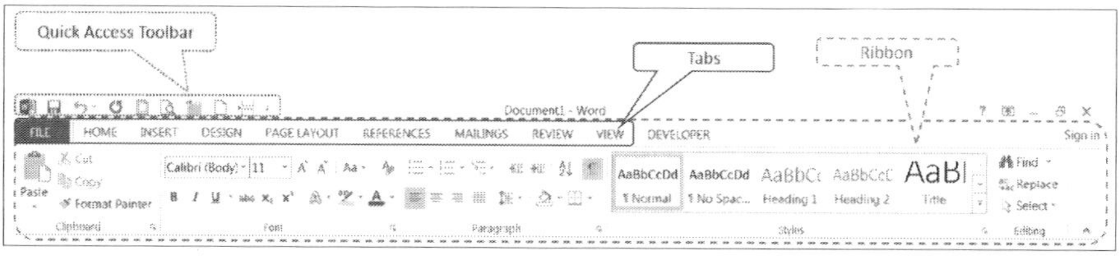

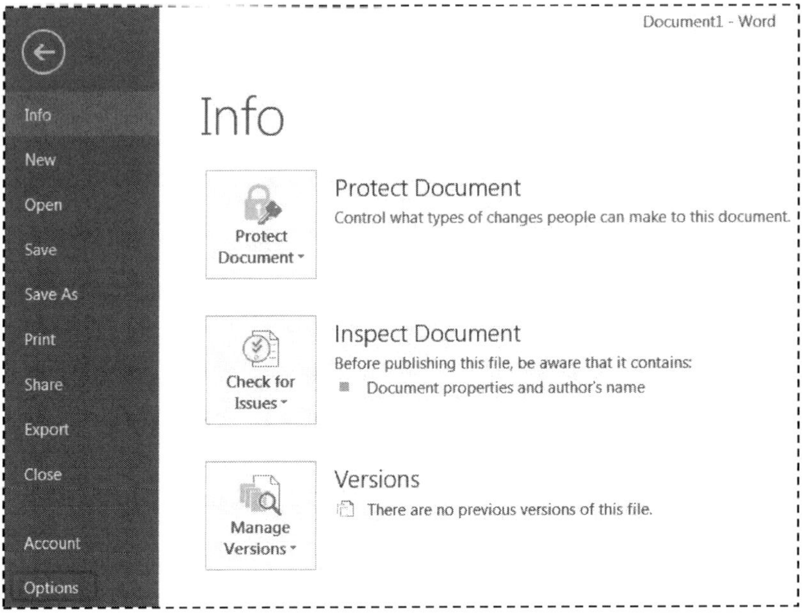

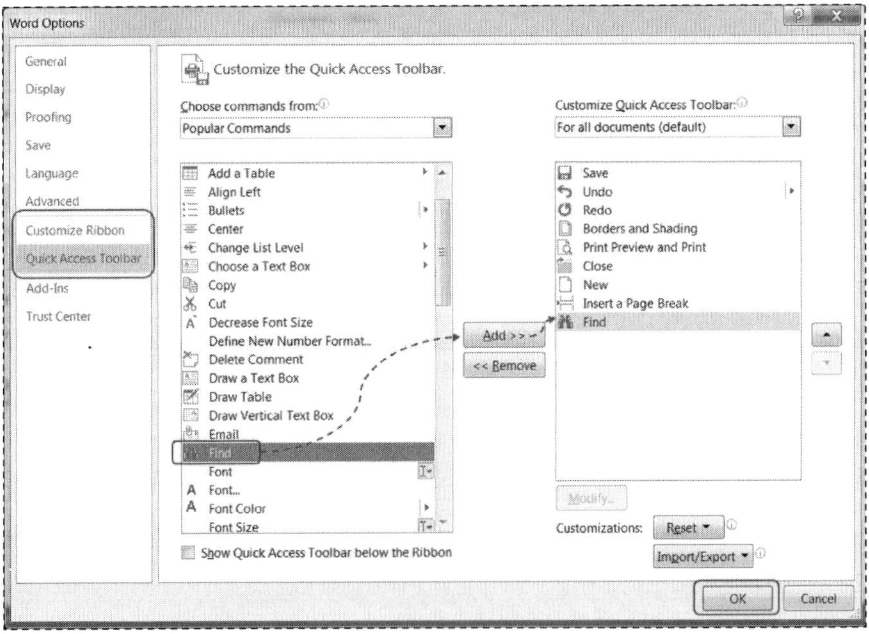

Lastly, across from the Quick Access Toolbar in the top left corner you'll notice a series of small icons.

Help Menu

The **? (question mark)**, when clicked, will launch the Microsoft® Word® **Help** menu, you may also press (**F1**) on your keyboard to access Help screen.

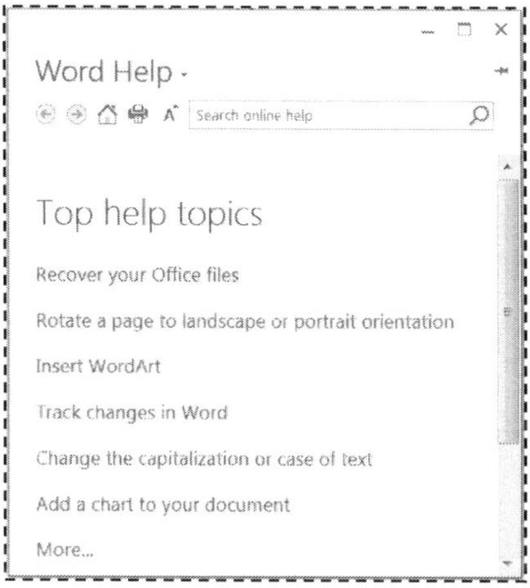

The  up arrow box button, when clicked, will present three Ribbon options:

1. **Auto-hide Ribbon** hides the Ribbon, until you click the top of worksheet to unhide
2. **Show Tabs** displays the tab name only, but not the commands
3. **Show Tabs and Commands** displays both the tab name and the commands *(this is the default setting)*

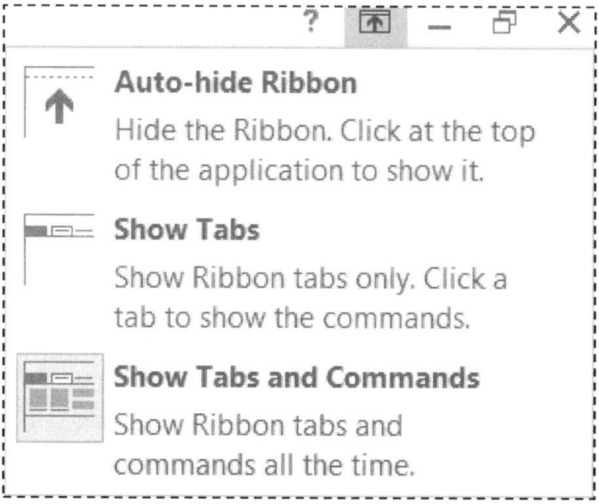

The  underscore button when clicked, will **minimize** the active document

The 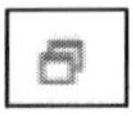 double window button when clicked, will **resize** the active document

The  cross (X) button when clicked, will **close** the active document (*you'll be prompted to save your file if not already done so)*

CHAPTER 3

Text Formatting & Saving A File

In Microsoft® Word® you can easily change the format of text, such as bolding, underling, or italicizing words in a document. This enables you to emphasize or highlight specific sections of importance. Similarly, by using bullets and numbers to list items, this helps to improve readability and comprehension of content.

In this chapter we'll review the seven most commonly used text formatting features available in Word®:

1. **Bold**
2. *Italic*
3. Underline
4. ~~strikethrough~~
5. Font styles & size increasing or decreasing
6. Text highlighting
7. Creating bulleted or numerated lists

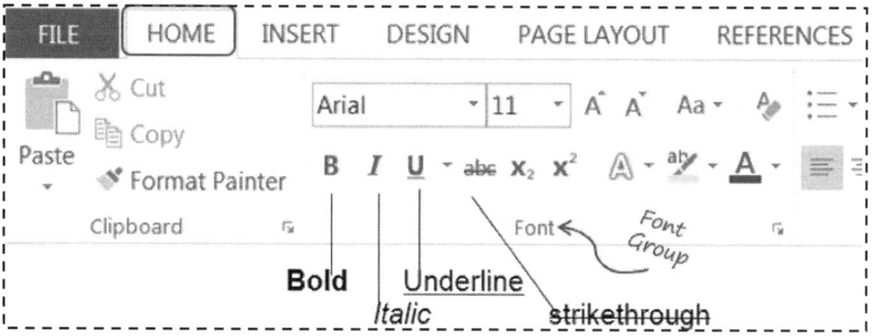

STEP-BY-STEP EXAMPLES:

Bold, Underline, Italic, & Strikethrough

1. Open Microsoft® Word® and create a new blank Word® document
   - From the Ribbon, Select **File: New: Blank document** *or*
   - Press shortcut keys **(CTRL + N)** on your keyboard

2. Type the following list of words:
   - Bold
   - Italic
   - Underline
   - strikethrough
3. Using your mouse, highlight (select) the word **'Bold'**
   - From the Ribbon select the **HOME** tab and the **Font** group
   - Click the letter **'B'** *or* press **CTRL+B** on your keyboard
4. Using your mouse, highlight (select) the word **'Italic'**
   - From the Ribbon select the **HOME** tab and the **Font** group
   - Click the letter ***'I'*** *or* press **CTRL+ I** on your keyboard
5. Using your mouse, highlight (select) the word **'Underline'**
   - From the Ribbon select the **HOME** tab and the **Font** group
   - Click the letter **'U'** *or* press **CTRL+U** on your keyboard
6. Using your mouse, highlight (select) the word **'strikethrough'**
   - From the Ribbon select **HOME** and the **Font** group
   - Click the letters **'~~abc~~'**

The list should appear similar to the following:

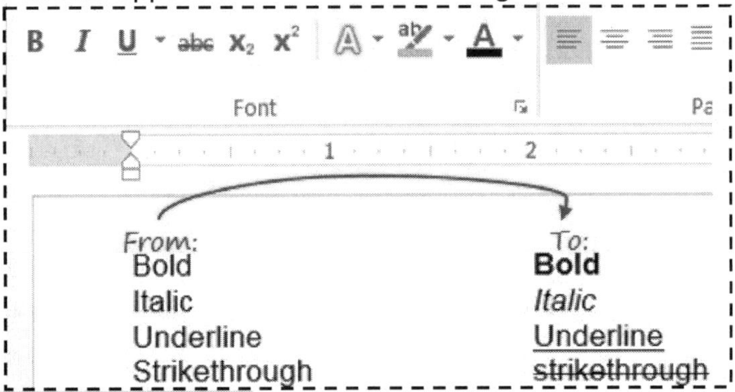

To remove the formatting, using your mouse, highlight (select) the word or words you wish to change and click the appropriate font button.

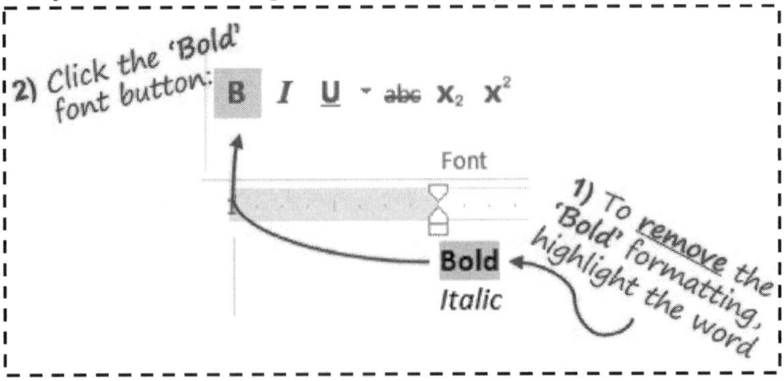

Font Types & Sizing

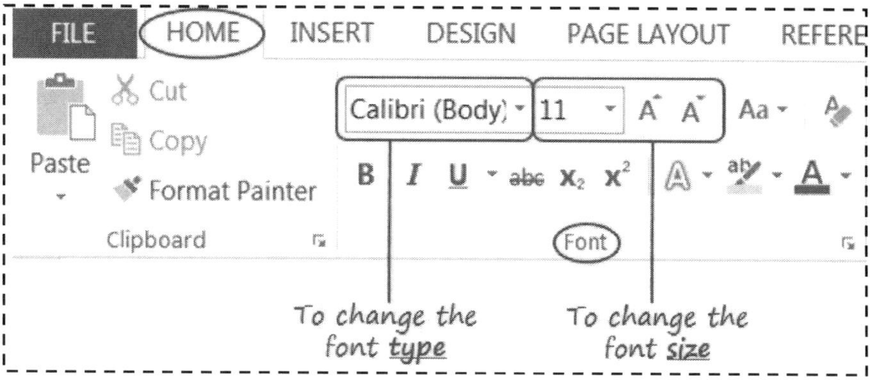

1. On a new line of the existing document, type the following list of words:
   - Courier New
   - increase
   - decrease
2. Using your mouse, highlight (select) the words **'Courier New'**
   - From the Ribbon select the **HOME** tab and the **Font** group
   - Click the **'font style'** drop-down list and select the font **'Courier New'**

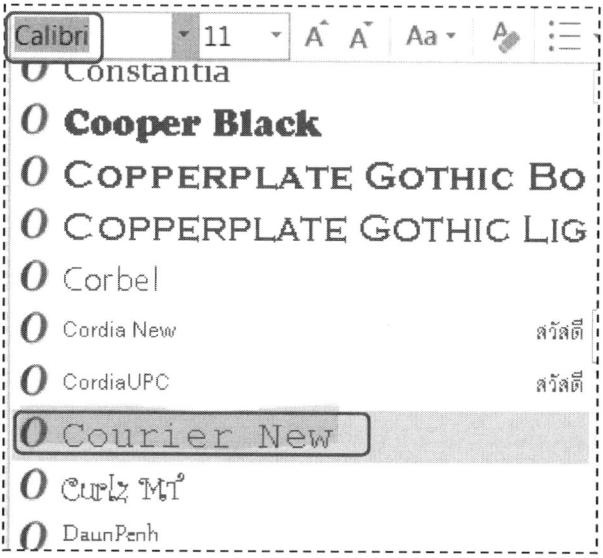

3. Using your mouse, highlight (select) the word **'increase'**
   - From the Ribbon select the **HOME** tab and the **Font** group
   - Click the **'font size'** drop-down list and select the number **'24'** _or_ click the symbol  until the font size 24 is reached

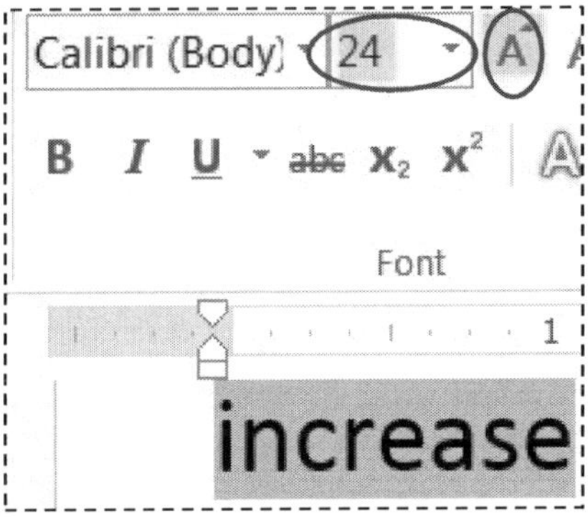

4. Using your mouse, highlight (select) the word **'decrease'**
   - From the Ribbon select the **HOME** tab and the **Font** group
   - Click the **'font size'** drop-down list and select the number **'8'** _or_ click the  symbol until the font size 8 is reached

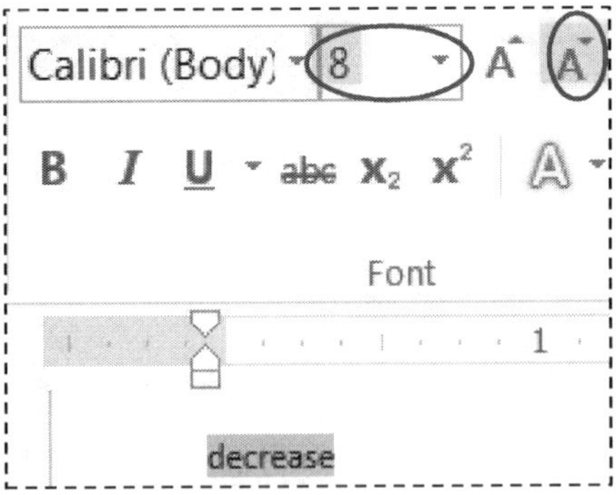

The list should appear similar to the following:

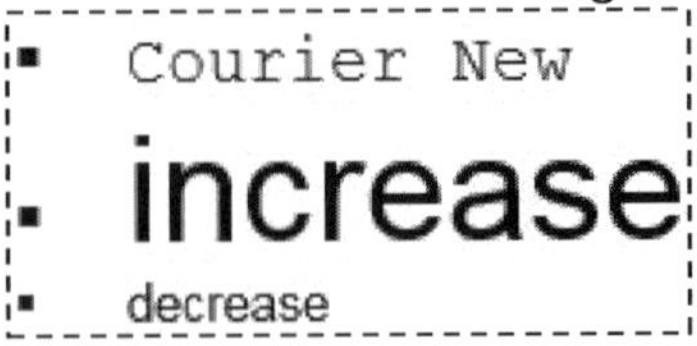

Text Highlighting

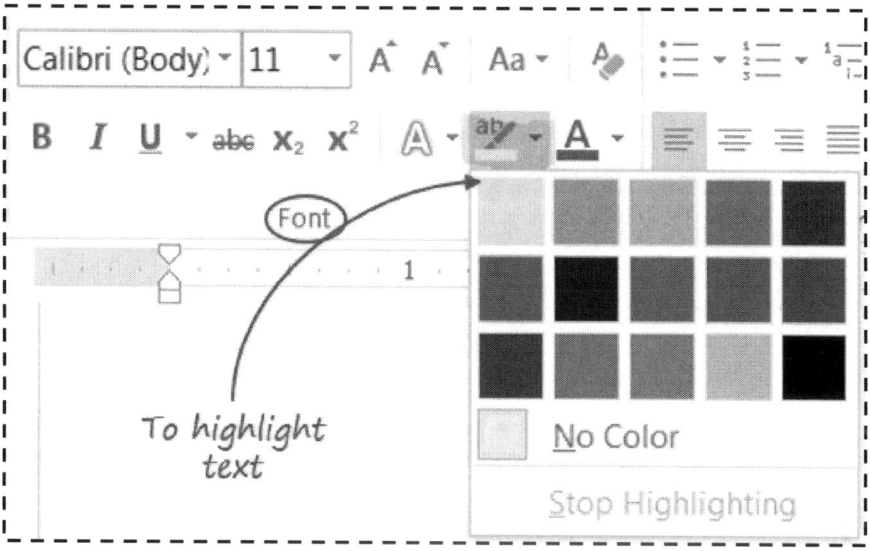

1. On a new line of the existing document, type the following words:
    - emphasize text
2. Using your mouse, highlight (select) the words **'emphasize text'**
    - From the Ribbon select the **HOME** tab and the **Font** group
    - Click the  symbol and select the shade yellow

The text should now be highlighted in yellow:

- emphasize text

ADDITIONAL INFORMATION:

You may also combine text highlighting and bolding to really emphasize the importance of content, for example:

> *"The following document describes the Sales department rules and regulations.* ***IMPORTANT*** *all employees must read."*

Bulleted and Numerated Lists

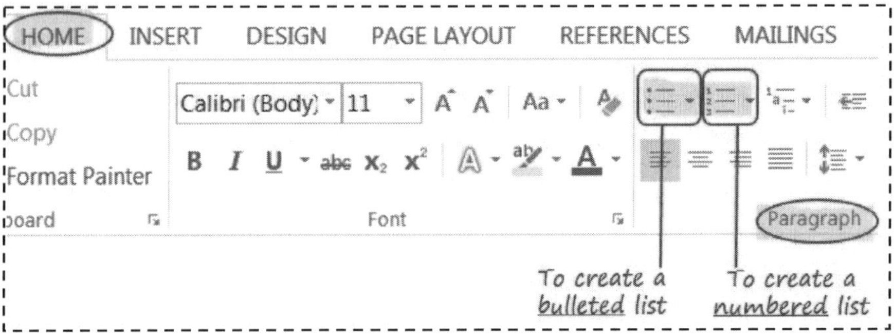

1. On a new line of the existing document, type the following list of words:
   Rule one
   Rule two
   Rule three
   Rule four

2. Using your mouse, highlight (select) the newly typed list of words
   - From the Ribbon select the **HOME** tab and the **Paragraph** group
   - Click the 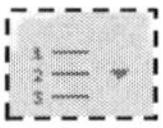 symbol and select the 1. 2. 3. option:

The list should now appear similar to the following:

1. Rule one
2. Rule two
3. Rule three
4. Rule four

Save

Before saving the file we just created, we first need to add a new folder in Windows® Explorer® called: **C:\WordTraining**

1. Click the *folder* icon  on the **'Start Task Bar'**

or

2. From the **'Start'** menu, select '**All Programs'**
   - Open the folder '**Accessories**'
   - Select the program **'Windows Explorer**'

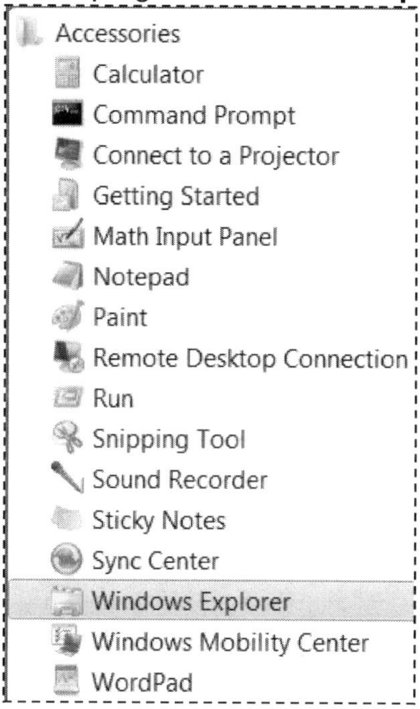

3. Once **'Windows Explorer**' is open:
   - Select the drive **C:**
   - Click **'New Folder'** from the toolbar

4. Name the newly created folder: **WordTraining**

5. Return to the **Word**® application and the document you just created:
   a. Click the **'Save'**  icon from the **'Quick Access Toolbar'**

or

- From the Ribbon, select the **'File'** tab
- Click the menu option **'Save As'**

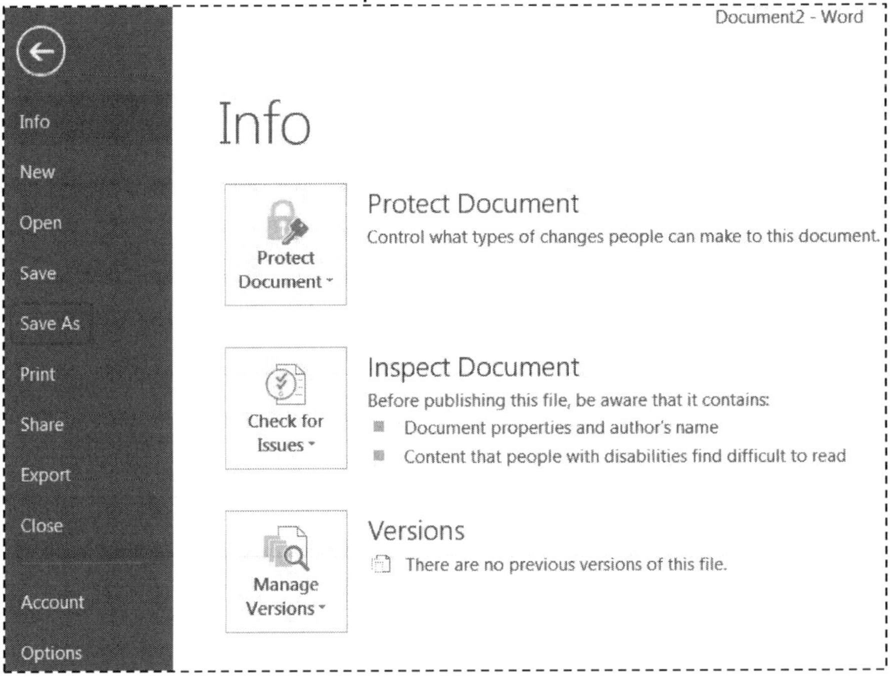

6. Click the **'Browse'** button

7. Select the **C:\WordTraining** folder

8. For **File name:** enter **TextFormatting.docx**
9. Click the '**Save**' button

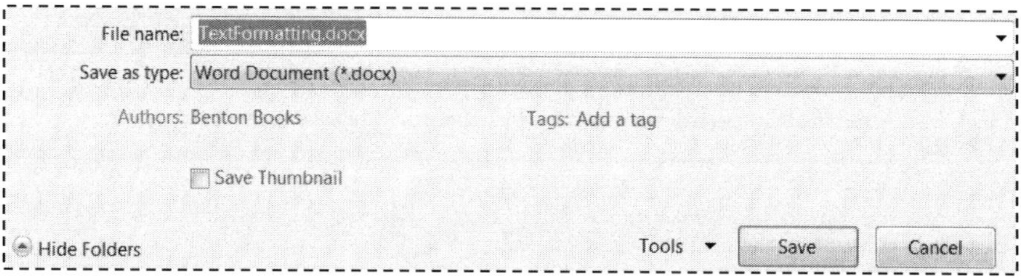

CHAPTER 4

Copy, Cut, Paste, & Format Painter

In this this chapter we review some the editing commands that allow us to quickly move content around a Word® document, these include:

- Copy, Cut, & Paste
- Format Painter

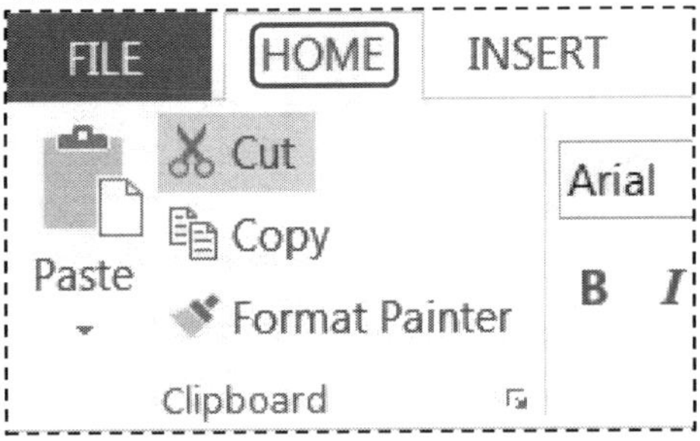

Copy

1. Open the file we created in Chapter 3 named: **TextFormatting.docx**
2. Using your mouse, highlight (select) the words `Courier New`
3. Click the **'Copy'**  button or press shortcut keys **CTRL+C** on your keyboard

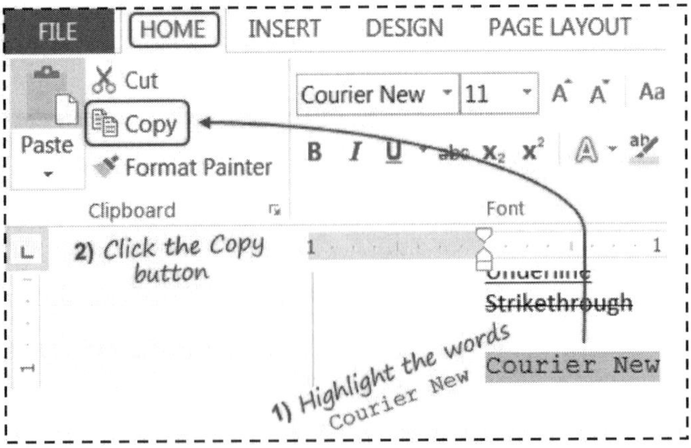

Paste

4. On a new line, click the **'Paste'** button or press shortcut keys **CTRL+V** on your keyboard

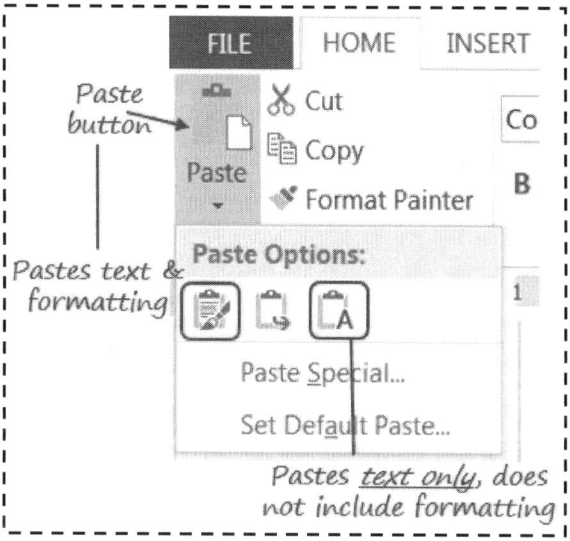

Cut

5. Using your mouse, highlight (select) the word increase
6. Click the **'Cut'**  button or press shortcut keys **CTRL+X** on your keyboard
7. On a new line, click the **'Paste'** button or press **CTRL+V** on your keyboard

---

Format Painter

The '**Format Painter**' allows you to replicate the same formatting from one piece of text, such as the font style and size and apply it to another piece of text.

1. Using your mouse, highlight (select) the word **Bold**
2. Click the **'Format Painter'**  button

3. Using your mouse *(the cursor should now be a paintbrush)*, highlight (select) the word increase

The word increase should now appear in smaller font and bold format:

Bold
Italic
Underline
~~Strikethrough~~

Courier New

~~decrease~~

emphasize text

1. Rule one
2. Rule two
3. Rule three
4. Rule four

Courier New
increase

4. You may close this file **without saving**

CHAPTER 5

Print & Creating A PDF (Portable Document File)

Next we'll demonstrate how to print documents and create a PDF (Portable Document File).

Print Preview

Before printing it is always helpful to first *preview* how your document appears. You may notice a page break or graphic in the preview and decide to adjust in the document's content to improve readability.

1. Open the file we created in Chapter 3 named: **TextFormatting.docx**

The three most common approaches to previewing a document are:

A. Click the **'Print Preview'** button, once added to your **'Quick Access Toolbar'** *(please see Chapter 2 for instructions on how to add commands to the Quick Access Toolbar)*

B. From the Ribbon, select the **'File'** tab, then the menu option **'Print'**

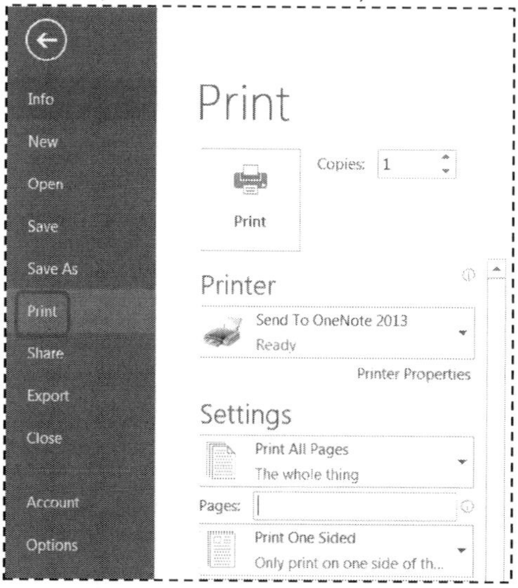

C. Press shortcut keys **CTRL+P** on your keyboard

Each of these options will allow you to *preview* the document, below is a screenshot of the print preview window:

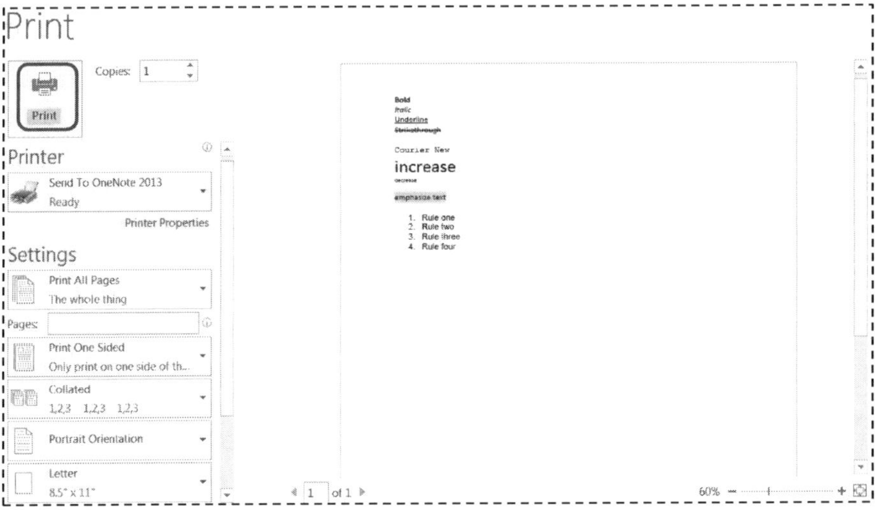

Print

2. If the preview is acceptable, click the **'Print'** button *(you will need to be connected to a printer)*

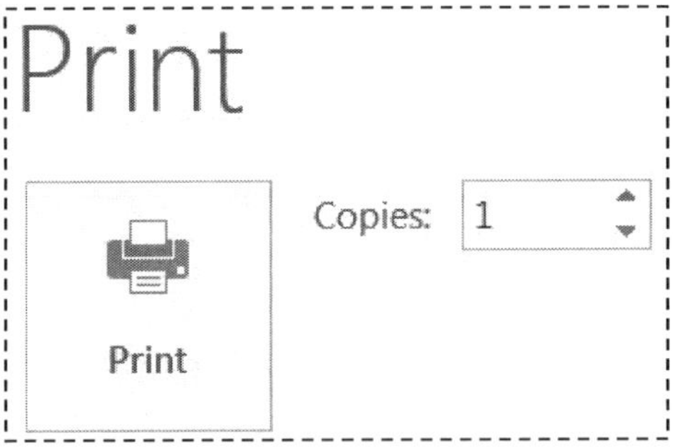

PDF (Portable Document File)

When you would like to distribute Word® documents to customers who may not have Microsoft® Word® installed on their computer or they may be viewing the content on a mobile device that does not support Office® files, being able to export your Word® documents is a useful alternative. A **P**ortable **D**ocument **F**ile or more commonly known as a **PDF,** converts your Word® content into a format that can be electronically transmitted and viewed with software developed to read PDFs. There are many PDF readers available, one of the most popular is Adobe® Acrobat® Reader®, which in many cases is free to download.

1. Open the file we created in Chapter 3 named: **TextFormatting.docx**
2. From the Ribbon, select the **'File'** tab, then the menu option **'Export'**

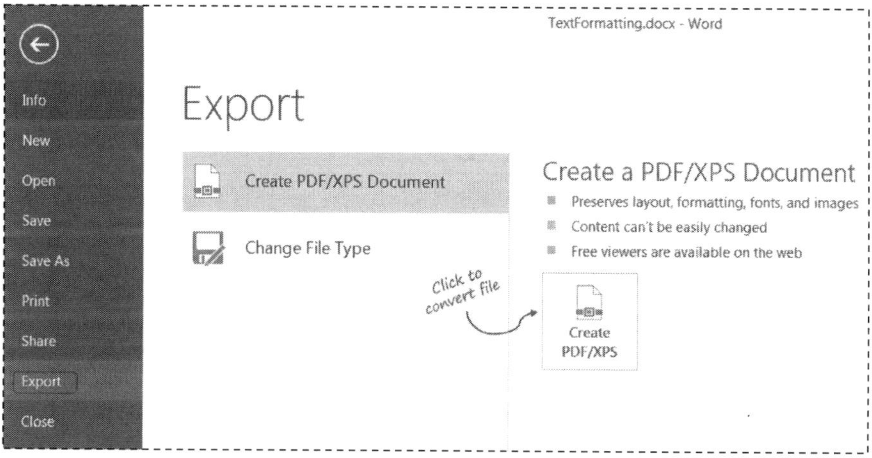

3. When prompted, click the **'Publish'** button

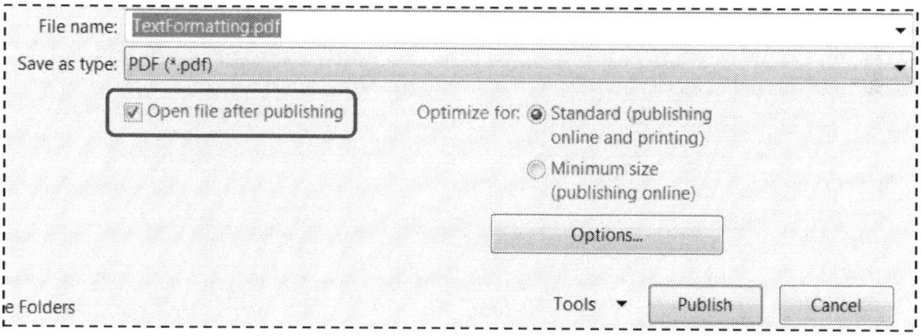

If you have a PDF reader installed on your computer the file will open, when the box *'Open file after publishing'* is checked. Otherwise, the file will be saved to the location you specified at the prompt, which is typically where the original Word® document is saved, in this case **C:\WordTraining**.

CHAPTER 6

Paragraph Indentation & Line Spacing

Often when a document contains a lot of text, readability can be improved by indenting the start of each new paragraph and changing the spacing between lines. This can be accomplished by adjusting the paragraph settings.

STEP-BY-STEP EXAMPLE:

1. Open Microsoft® Word® and create a new blank Word® document, press shortcut keys **(CTRL + N)**

2. Type and format the following lines of text:
    - **Document Presentation & Graphics Training**
    - Section 1 - Line Spacing & Margin
    - In this chapter we explore how to change paragraph line spacing and indention.

Increase the font size to 14
Document Presentation & Graphics Training
Section 1 - Line Spacing & Margins
In this chapter we explore how to change paragraph line spacing and indention.

3. Select (highlight) the following two rows of text:
    - Section 1 - Line Spacing & Margin
    - In this chapter we explore how to change paragraph line spacing and indention.

4. From the Ribbon **HOME** tab, *expand* the **Paragraph** group

Please see image on next page:

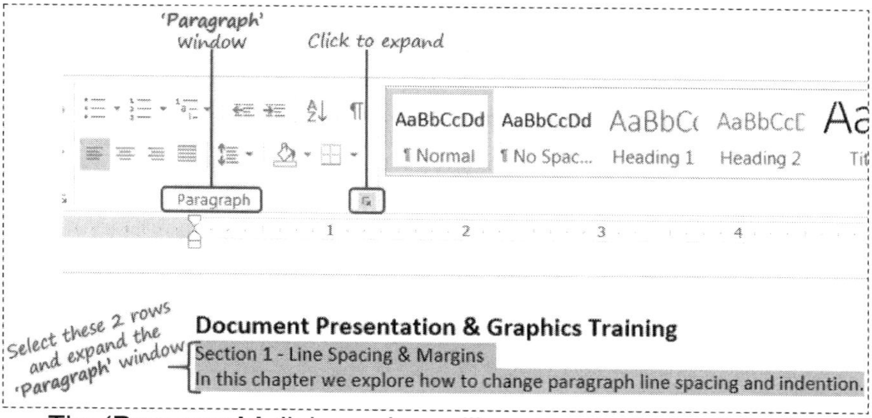

The **'Paragraph'** dialogue box will appear, to **'Indent'** the lines:

- Section 1 - Line Spacing & Margin
- In this chapter we explore how to change paragraph line spacing and indention.

5. Under the **'Indents and Spacing'** tab, click the **'Special:'** drop-down box and select **'First Line'**

6. To change the **'Line Spacing'**, click the **'Line spacing:'** drop-down box and select **'1.5 Lines'**

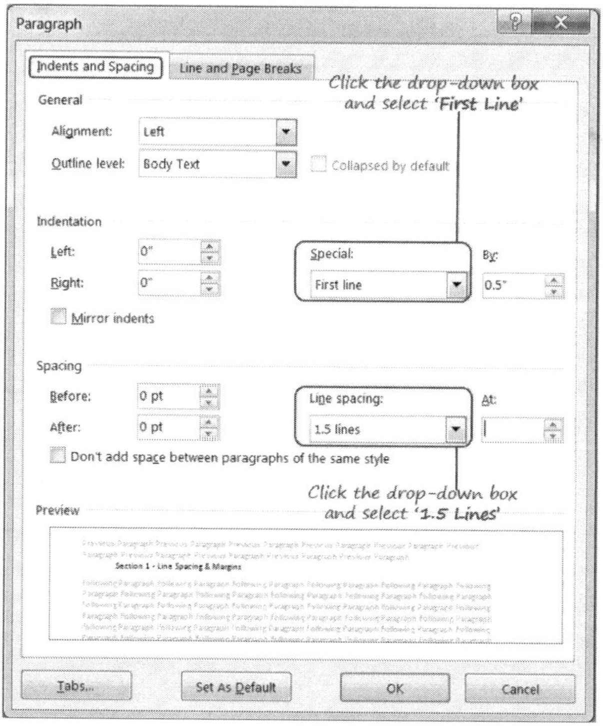

The following should now be displayed:

Document Presentation & Graphics Training
Spacing is now 1.5 lines between rows
Section is now indented
Section 1 - Line Spacing & Margin
In this chapter we explore how to change paragraph line spacing and indention.

7. Click the **'Save'** icon from the **'Quick Access Toolbar'**
   or
   - From the Ribbon, select the **'File'** tab
   - Click the menu option **'Save As'**
8. Click the **'Browse'** button
9. Select the **C:\WordTraining** folder
10. For **File name:** enter **PresentationAndGraphics.docx**
11. Click the '**Save**' button

CHAPTER 7

Page Breaks, Headers, Footers, & Page Numbers

Using Headers, Footers, and Page Numbers help give your Word® documents a professional appearance.

STEP-BY-STEP EXAMPLES:

Page Breaks

1. Open the file we created in Chapter 6 named: **PresentationAndGraphics.docx**
2. Type the following lines of text after the last sentence *"....line spacing and indention"*:
   - Section 2 – Page Breaks, Headers, & Footers (page numbers)
   - In this chapter we illustrate how to insert page breaks and add headers & footers.

Document Presentation & Graphics Training

Section 1 - Line Spacing & Margin

In this chapter we explore how to change paragraph line spacing and indention.

Section 2 – Page Breaks, Headers, & Footers (page numbers)

In this chapter we illustrate how to insert page breaks and add headers & footers.

Add the following 2 lines of text

3. Place your cursor in front the words **'Section 2'**
4. From the Ribbon select **INSERT : Page Break**
5. **Save** the file, press shortcut keys **(CTRL+S)** on your keyboard

Please see image on next page:

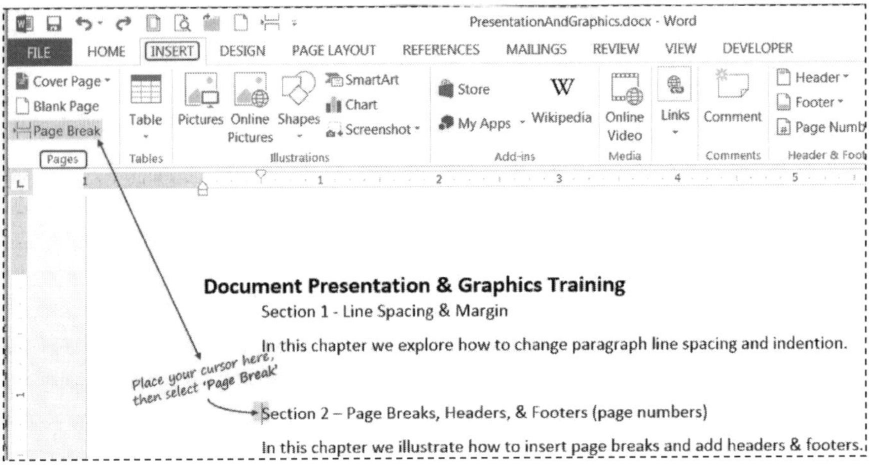

Headers

1. From the Ribbon select the **INSERT** tab
2. Click the drop-down box for '**Header**', in the **'Header & Footer'** section

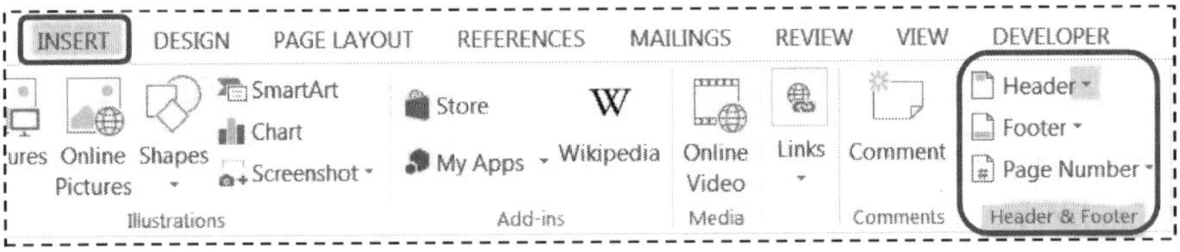

3. Scroll-down and select the option **'Alphabet'**, *if you do not see the option for **'Alphabet'**, select **'Banded'***

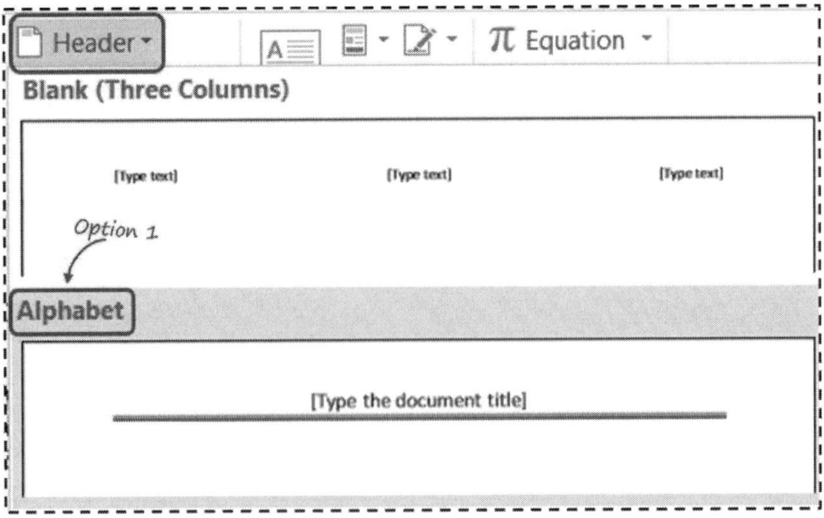

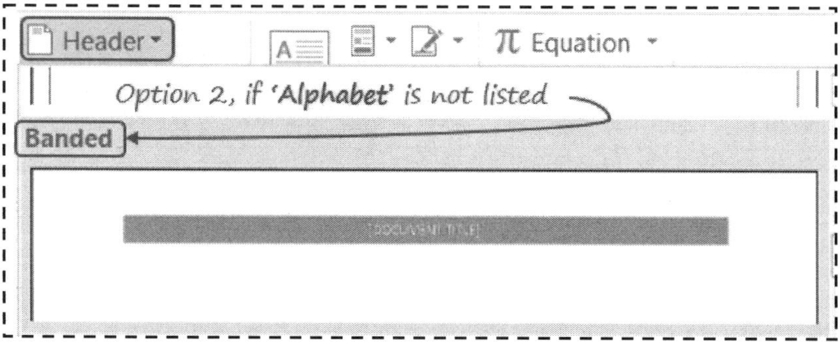

4. When prompted enter the following text for Title [Type the document title]:
    - Word Graphics and Presentation

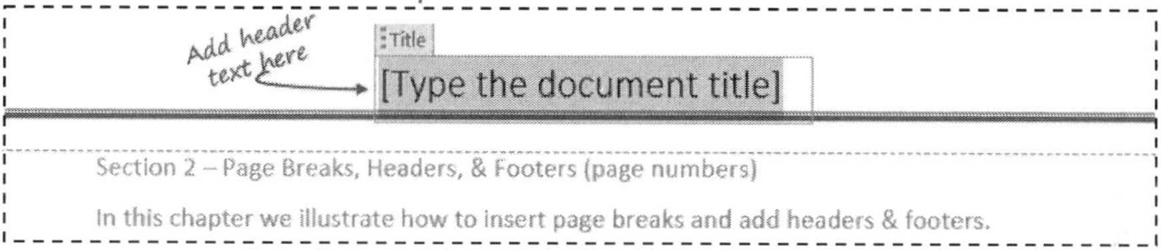

5. From the Ribbon, under the **HEADER & FOOTER TOOLS DESIGN** tab, click **'Close Header and Footer'**

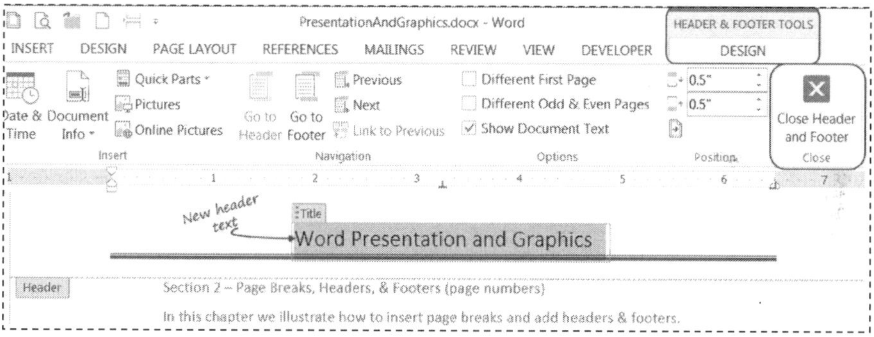

Footers

1. From the Ribbon select the **INSERT** tab
2. Click the drop-down box for '**Footer**', in the **'Header & Footer'** section

3. Scroll-down and select the option **'Facet (Odd Page)'**

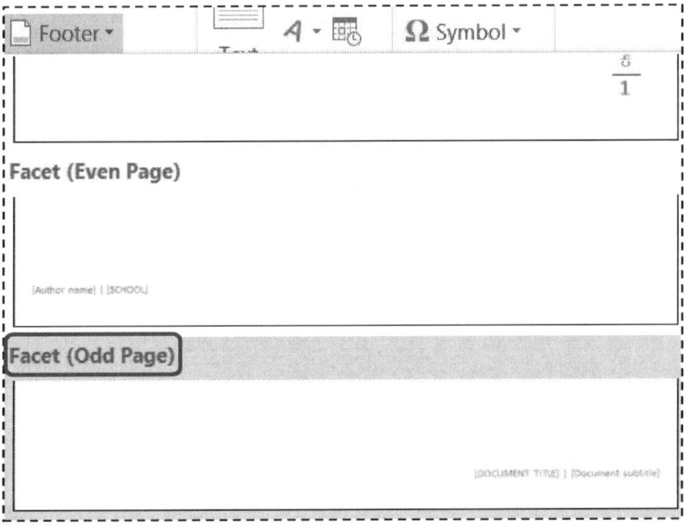

4. When prompted enter the following text for [Document subtitle]:
   - Word Training

5. From the Ribbon, under the **HEADER & FOOTER TOOLS DESIGN** tab, click **'Close Header and Footer'**

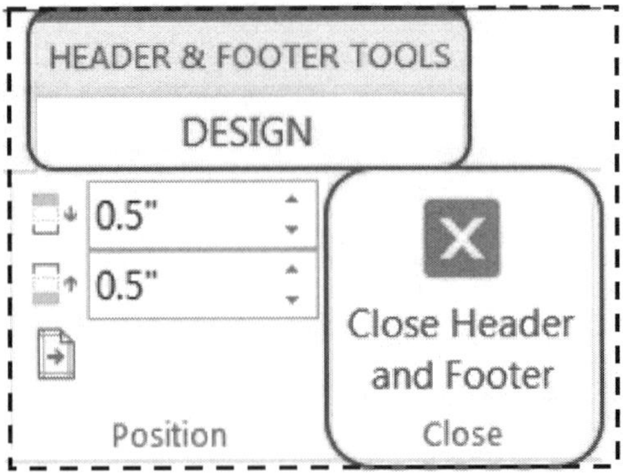

Page Numbers

1. From the Ribbon select the **INSERT** tab
2. Click the drop-down box for '**Page Number'**, in the **'Header & Footer'** section
3. Expand the menu for **'Bottom of Page'**
4. Scroll-down and select the option **'Bold Numbers 1'** under **Page X of Y**

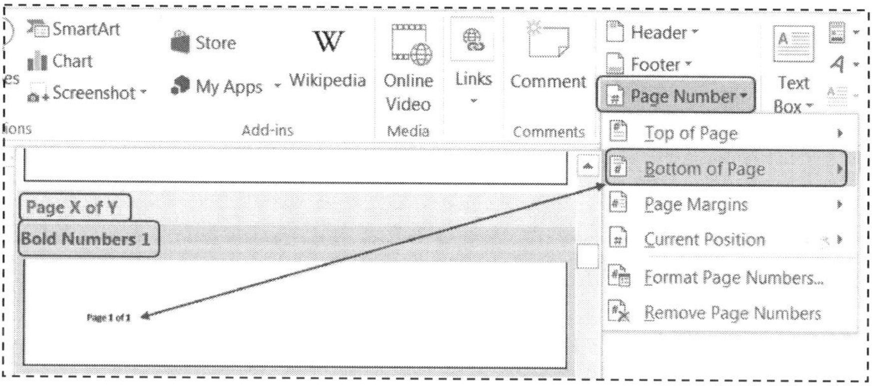

5. From the Ribbon, under the **HEADER & FOOTER TOOLS DESIGN** tab, click **'Close Header and Footer'**

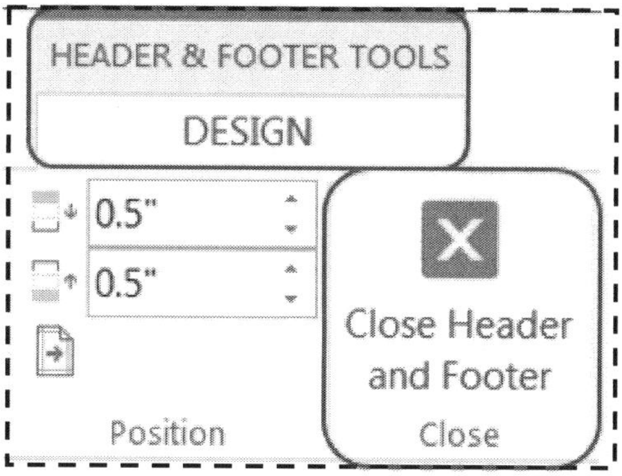

6. **Save** the **PresentationAndGraphics.docx** file

CHAPTER 8

Tables & Table Formatting

Tables are one of the most helpful features of Microsoft® Word® as they allow you to arrange similar information into a grid format such as:

- Names and addresses
- Sales, location, and product data
- Student and grade results
- Research subject and outcomes

This formatting improves understanding of subject matter and readability of documents.

STEP-BY-STEP EXAMPLES:

Inserting a Table (Grid)

1. Open the file we created in Chapter 3 named: **PresentationAndGraphics.docx**
2. Insert a page break *(for instructions on how to insert a page break, please see page 29)* after the word ***"...footers."*** on page 2 of the PresentationAndGraphics document
3. Type the following on the newly created page 3:
   - Section 3 – Tables
   - In this chapter we demonstrate how to insert and format a table.
4. On a new line, from the Ribbon select **INSERT : TABLE**, select **3 columns and 4 rows**

Please see image on next page:

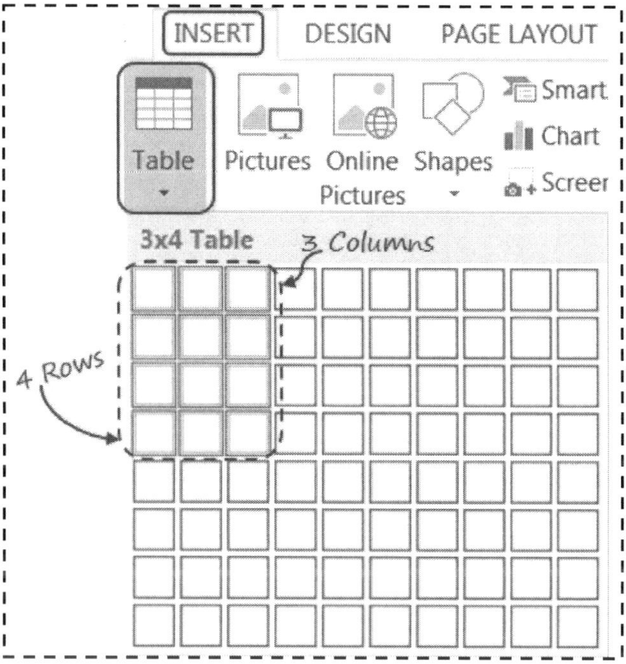

5. Enter the following headings in the first row of the table:
   - INSTRUCTOR
   - COURSE
   - ENROLLED

INSTRUCTOR	COURSE	ENROLLED

Add the following information:

INSTRUCTOR	COURSE	ENROLLED
Sally Winchester	Calculus 101	25
Peter Williams	Psychology 101	30
Robin Turner	Spanish 101	35

6. To reduce column width, select (highlight) all 3 columns
7. From the Ribbon, select the **'TABLE TOOLS : LAYOUT'** tab
8. For the **width Cell Size** enter **1.20"**

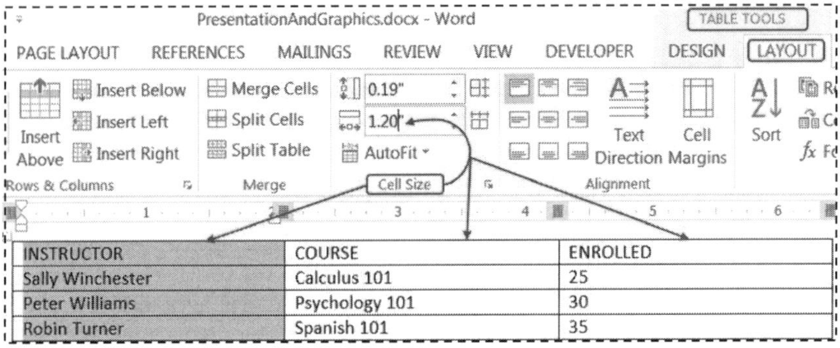

Formatting a Table

1. Highlight the first row, from the Ribbon select the **HOME** tab
2. From the *Font* group select **'B'** for **bold**
3. From the *Paragraph* group select the **center** icon

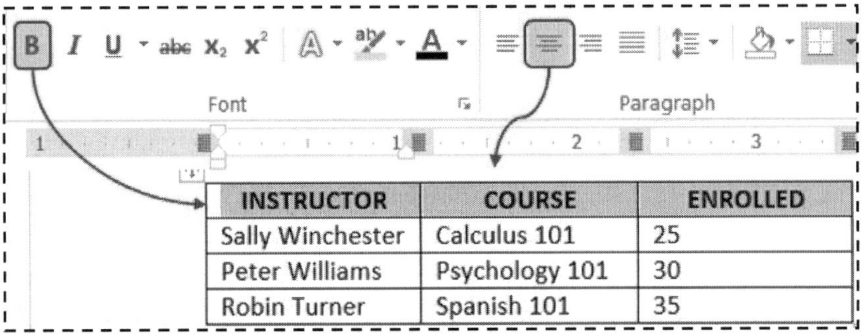

4. Place your cursor inside the first cell, with the word **'INSTRUCTOR'**
5. From the Ribbon, select the **'TABLE TOOLS : DESIGN'** tab
6. Expand the **'Table Styles'** window and select a style of your choice

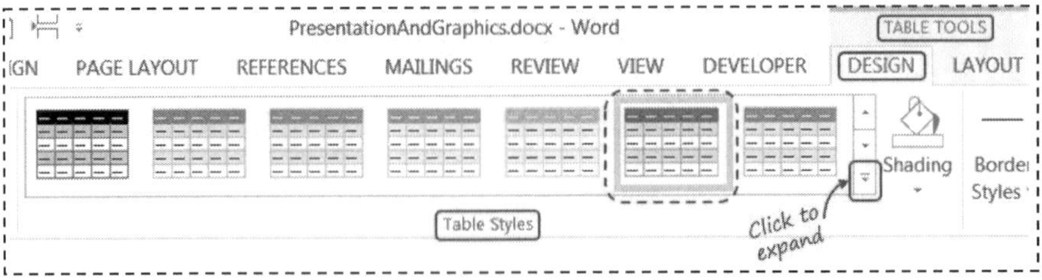

A table similar to the following should now be displayed:

INSTRUCTOR	COURSE	ENROLLED
Sally Winchester	Calculus 101	25
Peter Williams	Psychology 101	30
Robin Turner	Spanish 101	35

7. **Save** the **PresentationAndGraphics.docx** file

ADDITIONAL INFORMATION:

You may also create a table by selecting **INSERT : TABLE : Insert Table…**

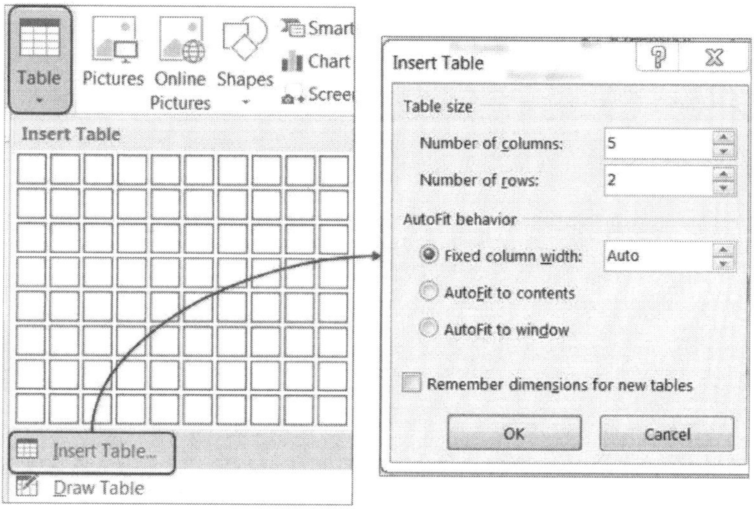

Inserting Additional Rows or Columns

To insert additional rows or columns into an existing table:

Option A: place your cursor in the *last row and column cell* and press the tab button on your keyboard

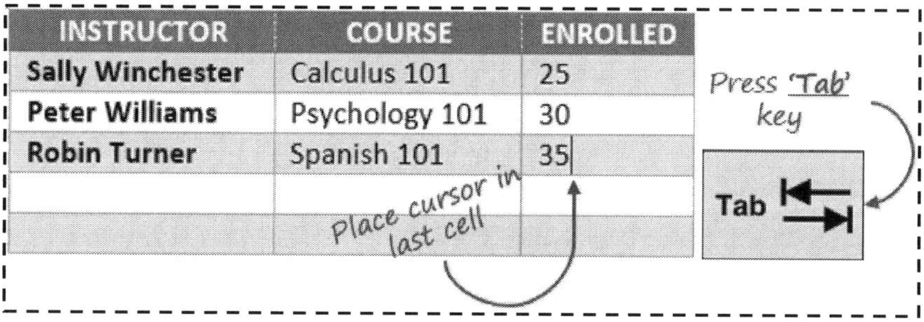

Option B: from the Ribbon, select the **'TABLE TOOLS : LAYOUT'** tab

- From the **'Rows & Columns'** section choose an option
  - Insert Above
  - Insert Below
  - Insert Left
  - Insert Right

Option C: place your cursor in the *last row and column cell* and **right-click** and choose an option

- Insert Above
- Insert Below
- Insert Left
- Insert Right

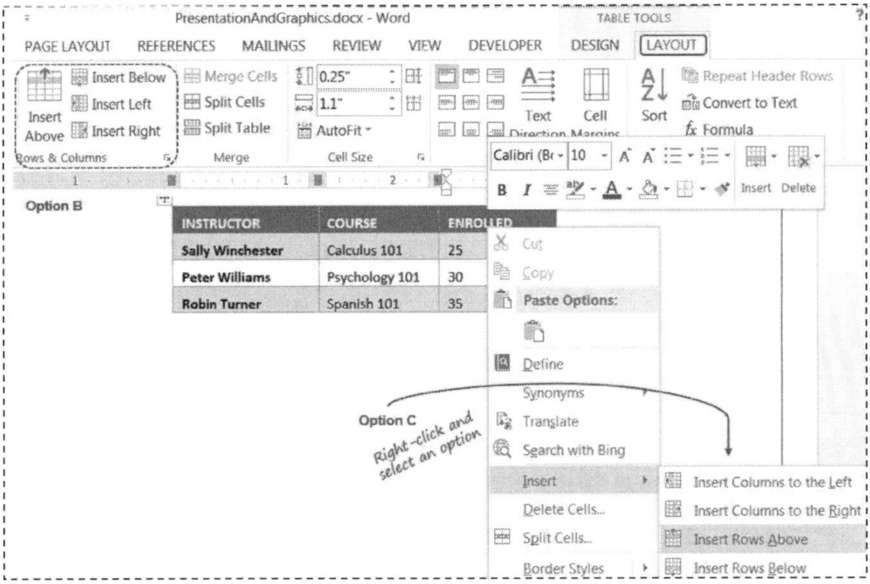

Deleting Rows or Columns

Option A: Highlight the rows or columns you want to remove

- From the Ribbon, select the **'TABLE TOOLS : LAYOUT'** tab
- From the **'Rows & Columns'** section click the **'Delete'** drop-down box and select an option
  - Delete Cells…
  - Delete Columns
  - Delete Rows
  - Delete Table

Option B: Highlight the rows or columns you want to remove, **right-click** and select either:

- Delete Rows
- Delete Columns

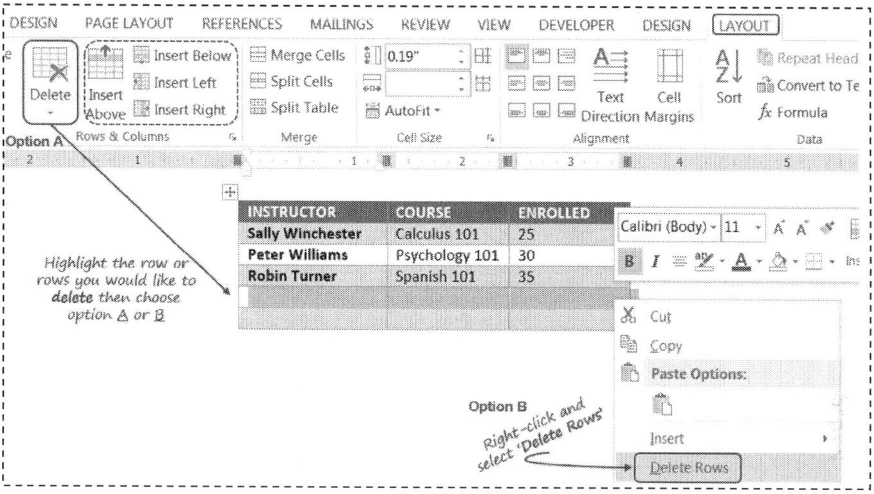

CHAPTER 9

Page Size & Orientation

There may be times when a document is more easily read in landscape vs. portrait format.

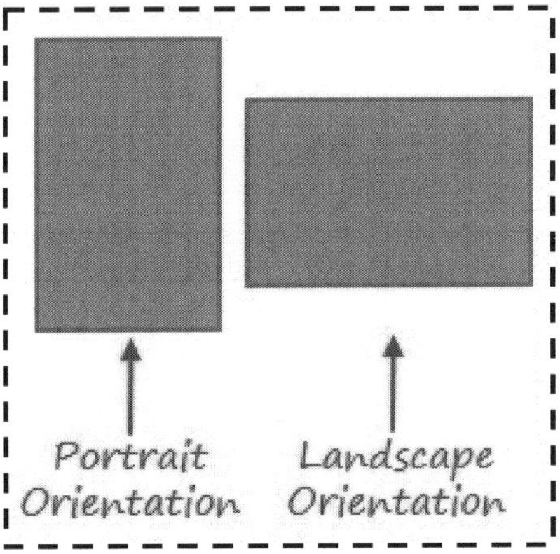

Similarly, the content you're presenting may be better represented on different size paper, for example legal size (8.5" W x 14" L) instead of the standard letter size (8.5" W x 11" L).

STEP-BY-STEP EXAMPLE:

Landscape vs. Portrait format

1. Open the file we created in Chapter 3 named: **PresentationAndGraphics.docx**
2. Insert a page break *(for instructions on how to insert a page break, please see page 29)* after the ***table*** on page 3 of the PresentationAndGraphics document
3. Type the following on the newly created page 4:
   - Section 4 – Page Size & Orientation
   - A demonstration on changing the page orientation to landscape.

4. On a new line, from the Ribbon select the tab **PAGE LAYOUT**
5. Click the drop-down box for **'Orientation'** and select the **'Landscape'** option.

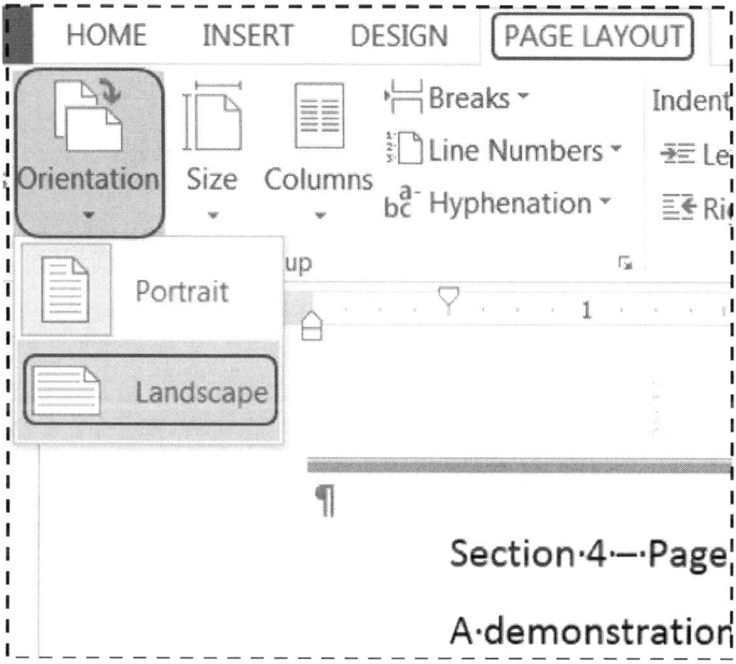

Note: how the PresentationAndGraphics document is now in landscape or wide format.

6. Press shortcut keys **CTRL+Z** *(undo last command)* on your keyboard to change back the orientation to portrait

---

Paper size legal vs. letter

1. From the Ribbon select the tab **PAGE LAYOUT**
2. Click the drop-down box for **'Size'** and select the **'`Legal 8.5"`** **`x 14"`'** option

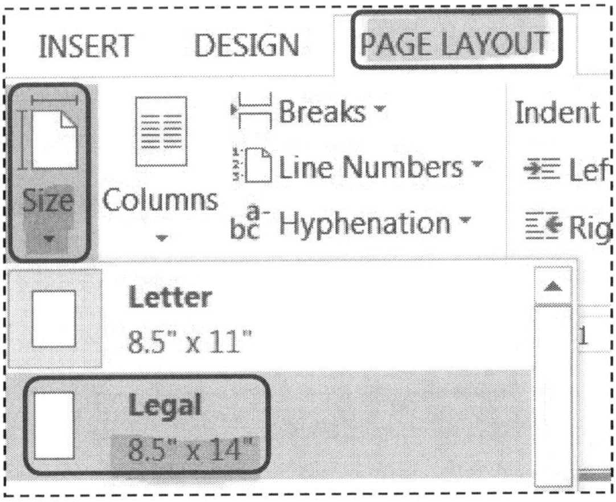

Note: how the PresentationAndGraphics document is now in legal size page length (8.5” W x 14” L).

3. Press shortcut keys **CTRL+Z** *(undo last command)* on your keyboard, to change back the page size back to portrait or standard letter size (8.5” W x 11” L)
4. You <u>do not</u> need to save this exercise

CHAPTER 10

SmartArt & Shapes

Shapes and SmartArt enhance your documents by providing modifiable graphics which may be used to:

- Highlight or call-out important aspects of your document
- Direct users to additional information or materials
- Illustrate hierarchical relationships
- Describe a process flow

STEP-BY-STEP EXAMPLE:

SmartArt

1. Open the file we created in Chapter 6 named: **PresentationAndGraphics.docx**
2. Insert a page break *(for instructions on how to insert a page break, please see page 29)* after the word ***"landscape."*** on page 4 of the PresentationAndGraphics document
3. Type the following on the newly created page 5:
   - Section 5 – SmartArt & Shapes
4. On a new line, from the Ribbon select the tab **INSERT**
5. Click the **'SmartArt'** button

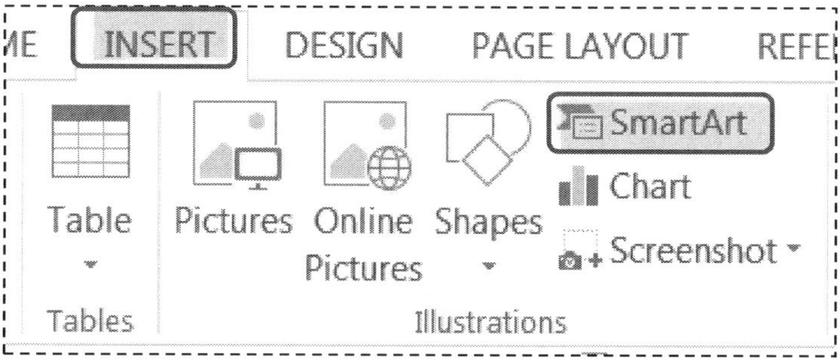

The following dialogue box will appear.

6. Scroll-down until you reach the **'Hierarchy'** section and select the **'Half Circle Organization Chart'**
7. Click the **'OK'** button

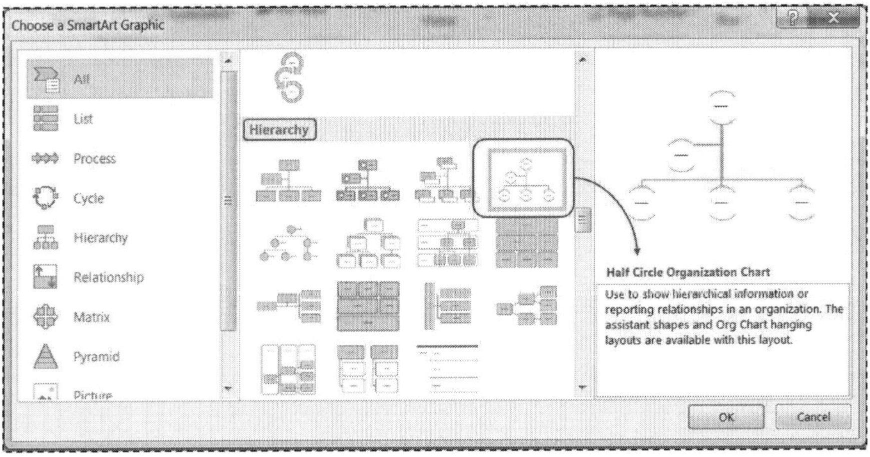

The following should now be displayed on page 5 of the **PresentationAndGraphics** document:

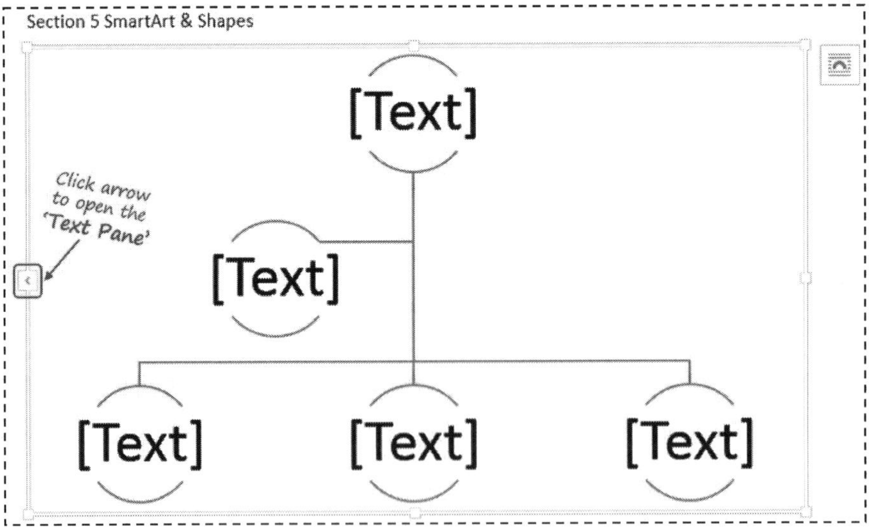

8. Click the arrow to open the **'Text Pane'**

9. Type **'Developer'** into the *first* [Text] box of the **'Text Pane'**
10. Type **'Builder'** into the *second* [Text] box of the **'Text Pane'**

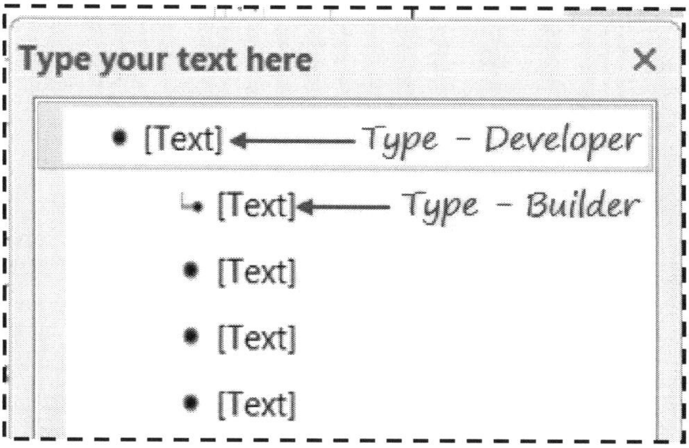

11. Place your cursor after the word **'Builder'** and press the **'Enter ←'** button on your keyboard
12. Type the word **'Agent'** into the *third* [Text] box of the **'Text Pane'**

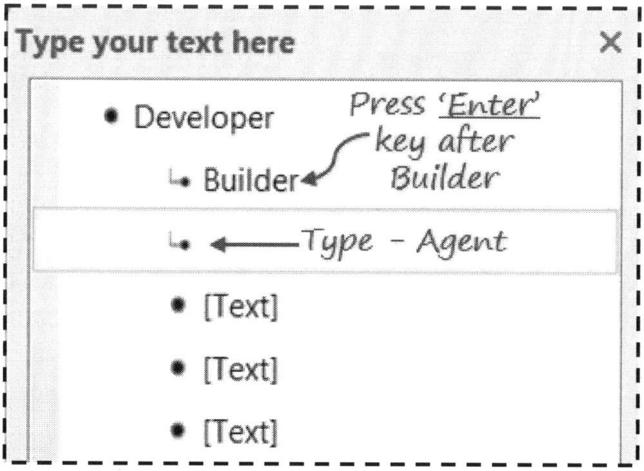

13. Type **'Buyer'** in the *fourth* [Text] box of the **'Text Pane'**
14. Place your cursor before the word **'Buyer'** and press the **'Tab'** button on your keyboard

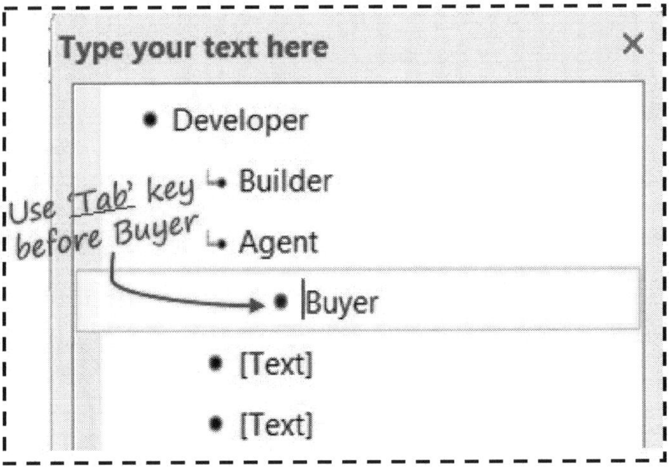

15. Using the **'BACK SPACE ←'** button on your keyboard remove the remaining two [Text] boxes of the **'Text Pane'**

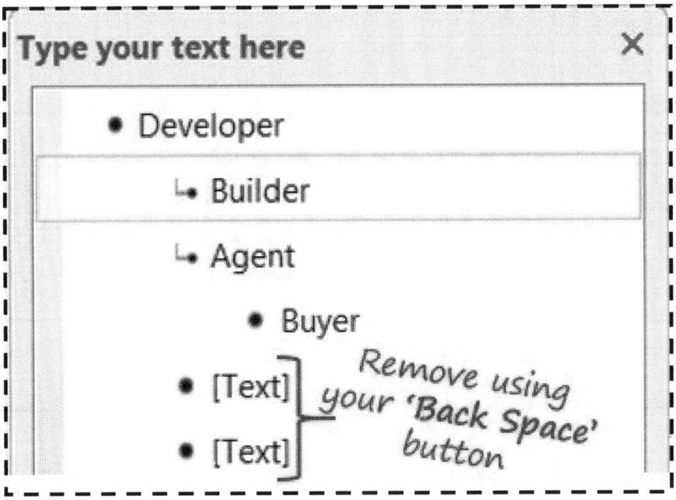

16. Place your cursor after the word **'Builder'** and press the **'Enter ←'** button on your keyboard twice
17. Enter the text **'Sub-Contractor'** in each of the two newly added levels

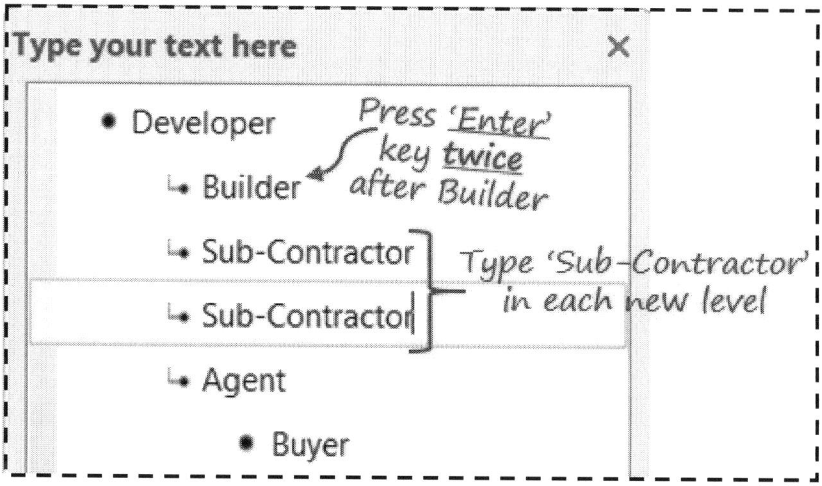

18. Place your cursor before each the words **'Sub-Contractor'** and press the **'Tab'** button on your keyboard

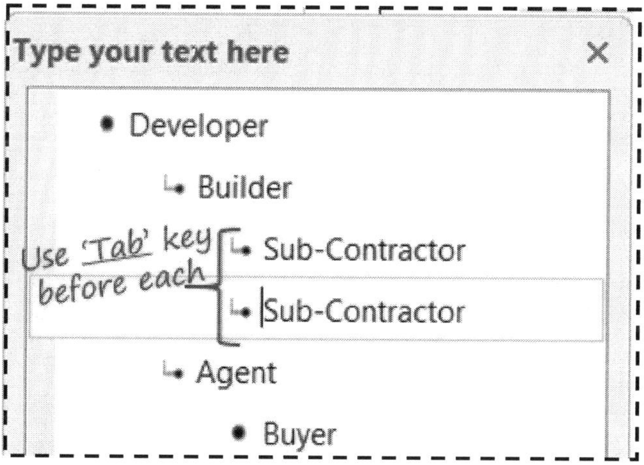

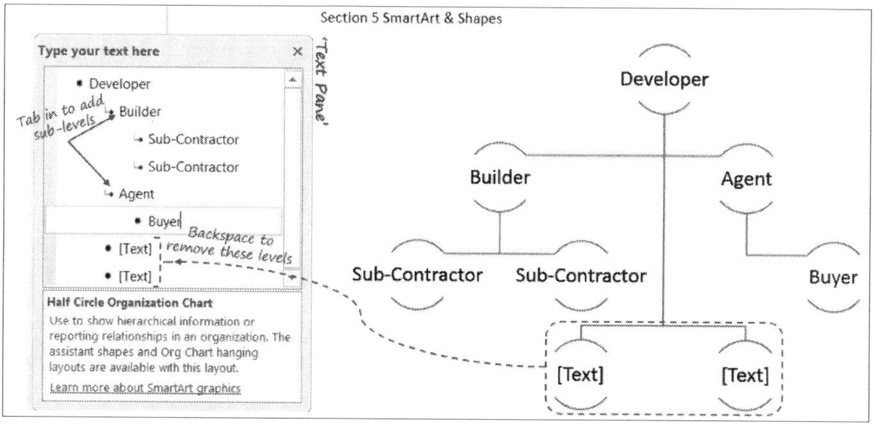

You may also change the layout, by selecting the **'DESIGN'** tab from the **'SMARTART TOOLS'** Ribbon and then **'Layouts'**:

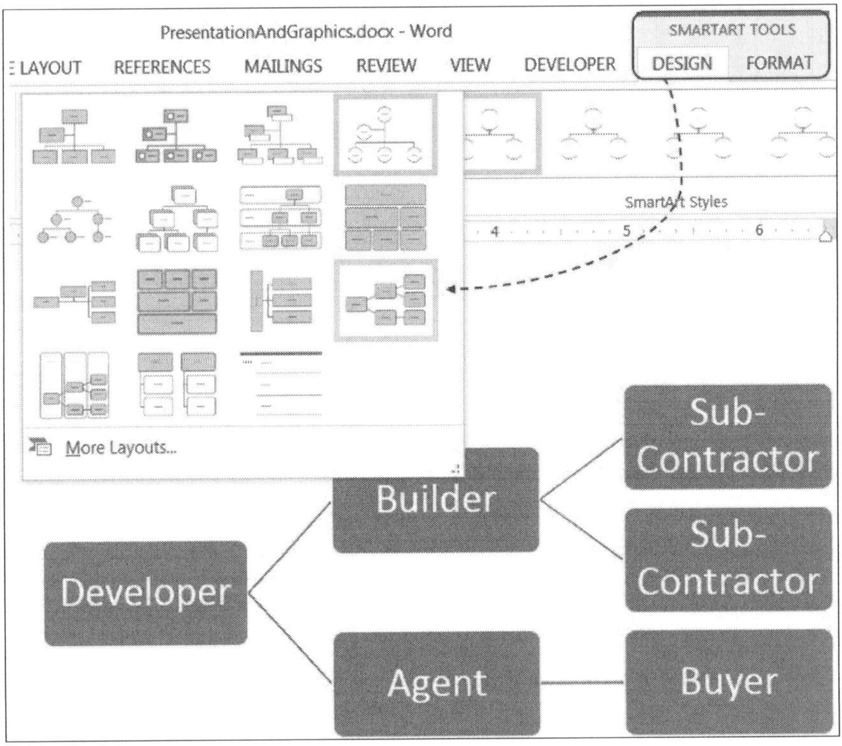

Shapes

To insert a shape:

1. From the Ribbon select the tab **INSERT**
2. Click the **'Shapes'** drop-down button
3. Click the first **'Callout'** option

Please see image on next page:

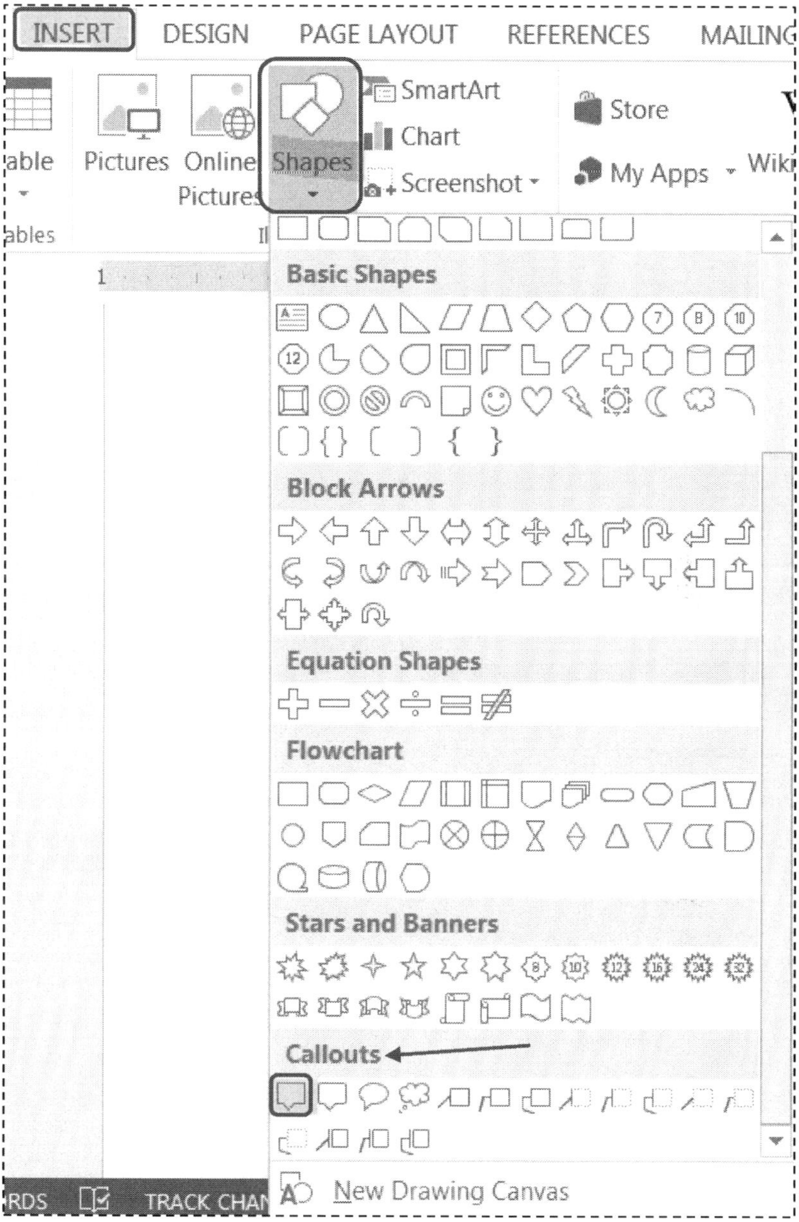

4. The cross symbol + will be displayed, allowing you to *draw* in the location you wish to place the callout. Draw near the word **'Agent'**
5. Click inside the callout and type the text **'Open Position'**
6. **Save** the **PresentationAndGraphics.docx** file

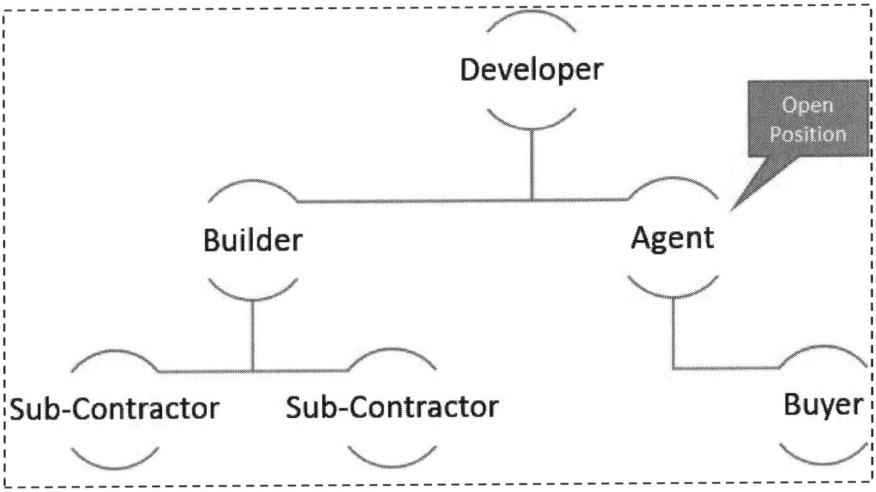
Developer
Open Position
Builder
Agent
Sub-Contractor
Sub-Contractor
Buyer

CHAPTER 11

Screenshots / Screen Clipping

Screenshots or screen clips are an effective means in which to improve comprehension of your document. They also communicate content more quickly and may be used instead of or in addition to text.

STEP-BY-STEP EXAMPLE:

1. Close all other programs you have open on your computer
2. Open the file we created in Chapter 6 named: **PresentationAndGraphics.docx**
3. Scroll down to page 5, **'Section 5 SmartArt & Shapes'**
4. Create a **new blank Word® document (CTRL + N)**
5. In the **new document** type the following line of text:
   - `Example of a screenshot`
6. On a new line, from the Ribbon select the **INSERT** tab
7. From the **'Illustrations'** group, click the **drop-down arrow** for **'Screenshot'**
8. Select the **'Screen Clipping'** option

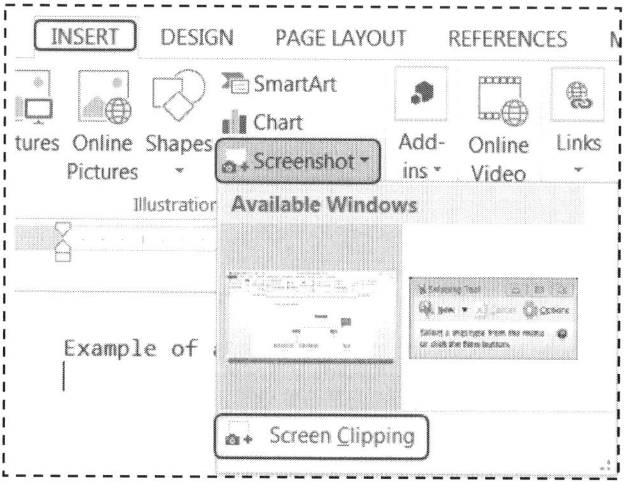

9. Your screen will appear with a transparent white background, and the cross symbol + will be displayed
10. Your screen will change and should display page 5, **'Section 5 SmartArt & Shapes'** of the **PresentationAndGraphics** document

The cross symbol allows you to select a portion of the image you want screen capture.

11. Using the cross symbol + hold the left mouse button and **drag to select** the **'Section 5 SmartArt & Shapes'** section

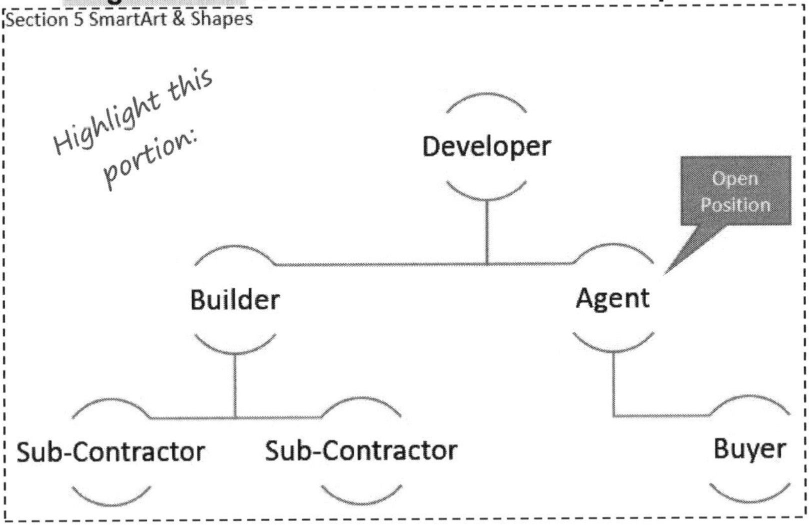

The screenshot should now appear in the **new document:**

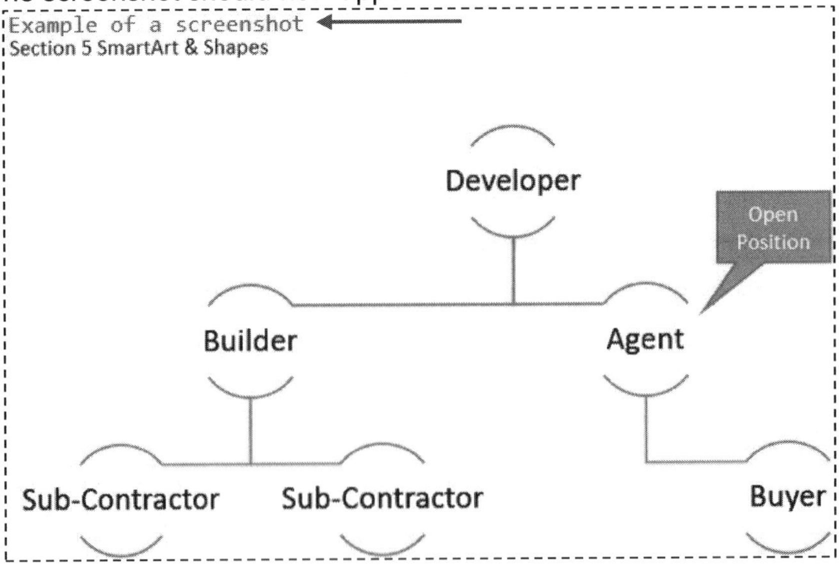

12. You may close both files **without saving**

ADDITIONAL INFORMATION:

If you have multiple windows open, click the window you want to capture ***before*** starting the screenshot process. This will move that window to be the active file when selecting the **'Screen Clipping'** option.

If the file containing the image you want to take the screenshot of is large, you will need to scroll-down to the section of the document that contains the portion you want to capture ***before*** selecting the **'Screen Clipping'** option.

CHAPTER 12

Table Of Contents

In addition to making your documents look professional, providing a Table of Contents adds helpfulness, by allowing your audience to easily go to a specific pages of interest.

STEP-BY-STEP EXAMPLE:

1. Open the file we created in Chapter 6 named: **PresentationAndGraphics.docx**
2. On page 1, using your mouse select the line
   - Section 1 - Line Spacing & Margin
3. From the Ribbon **HOME** tab, under the **Styles** group, select **'Heading 2'**

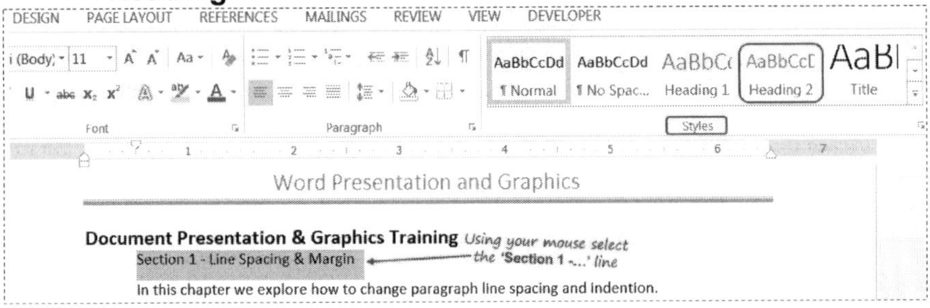

4. Repeat steps 2 & 3 for *all five* sections of the **PresentationAndGraphics** document. All should now be **'Heading 2'**

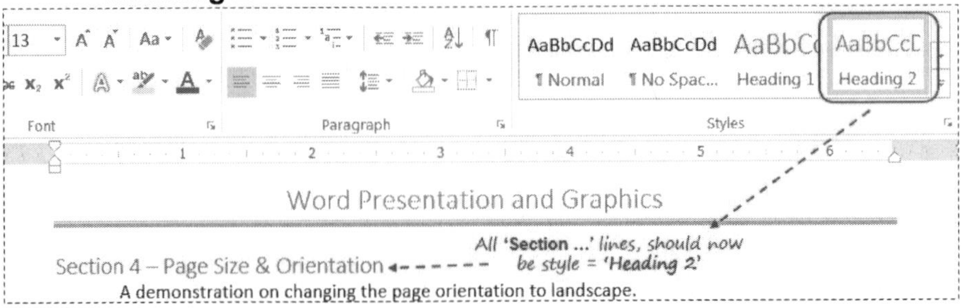

5. From the Ribbon select the **VIEW** tab, and click the **'Navigation Pane'** check box

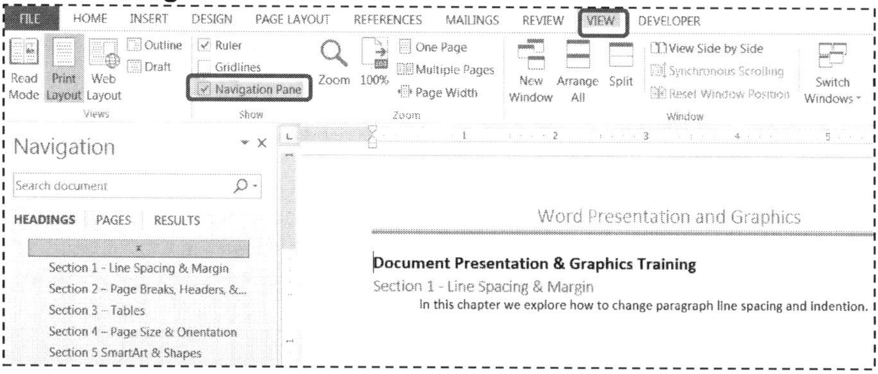

6. On page 1, place your cursor before the line **Document Presentation & Graphics Training**

7. Insert a Page Break *(for instructions on how to insert a page break, please see page 29)*

8. On the new page 1, from the Ribbon select the **REFERENCES** tab, and click the drop-down box for **'Table of Contents'**

9. Select the option **'Automatic Table 2'**

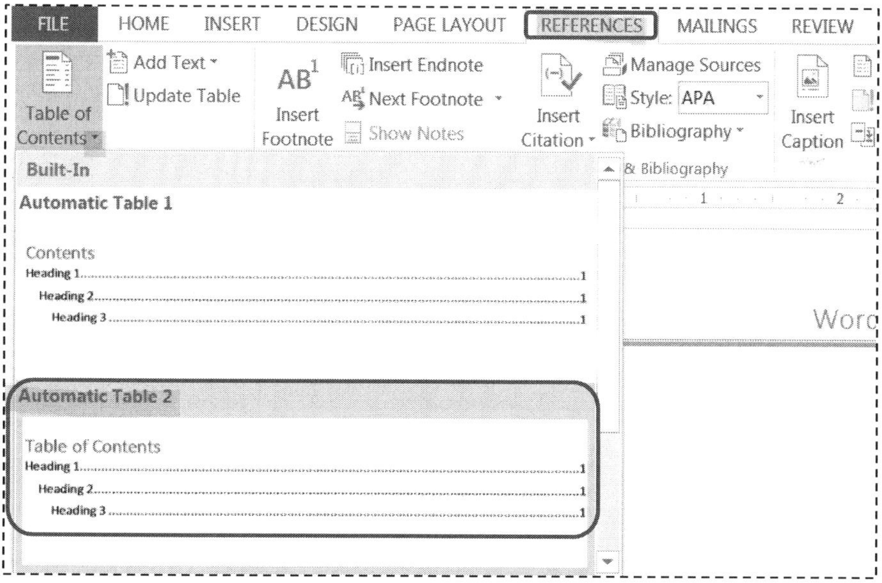

The following Table of Contents should now be displayed on page 1

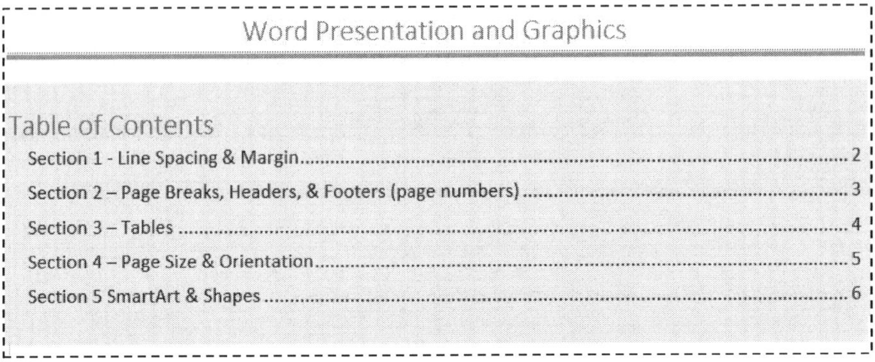

10. **Save** the **PresentationAndGraphics.docx** file

Removing a Table of Contents

- To remove a Table of Contents, from the Ribbon select the **REFERENCES** tab
- Click the drop-down box for **'Table of Contents**'
- Select **'Remove Table of Contents'**

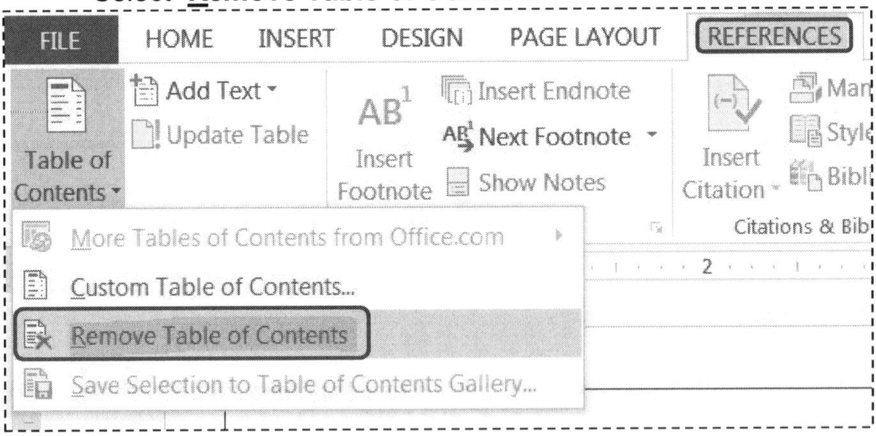

CHAPTER 13

Document Formatting & Page Borders

In the previous lessons we learned how to do our own formatting, however Microsoft® Word® also provides built-in design formats and the ability to add page borders to give your documents a sophisticated look.

STEP-BY-STEP EXAMPLES:

Word® Document Formats

1. Open the file we created in Chapter 6 named: **PresentationAndGraphics.docx**
2. From the Ribbon select the **DESIGN** tab, and expand the **'Document Formatting'** box

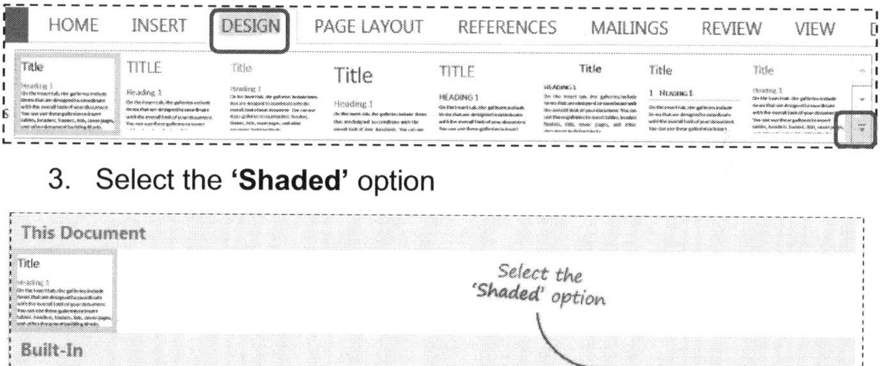

3. Select the **'Shaded'** option

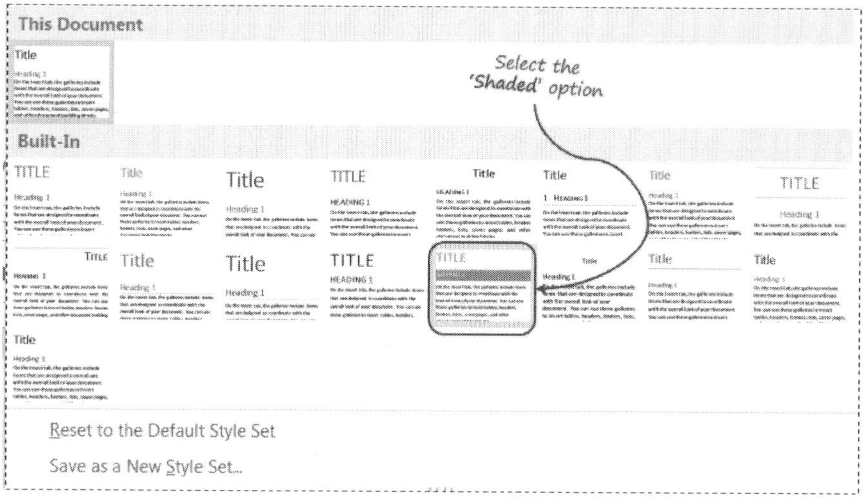

Formatting similar to the following should now be displayed:

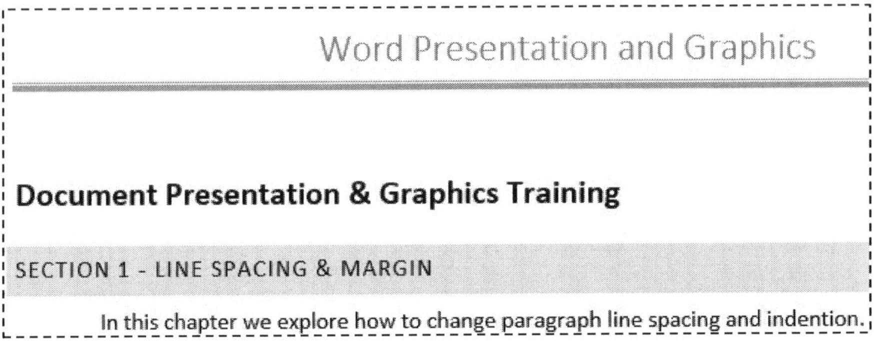
Word Presentation and Graphics
Document Presentation & Graphics Training
SECTION 1 - LINE SPACING & MARGIN
In this chapter we explore how to change paragraph line spacing and indention.

Page Borders

1. From the Ribbon select the **DESIGN** tab
2. Click the **'Page Borders'** icon
3. Once the **'Borders and Shading**' dialogue box opens, select the **'Box'** option
4. Optionally, you may change the color or line style of the border
5. Click the **'OK'** button

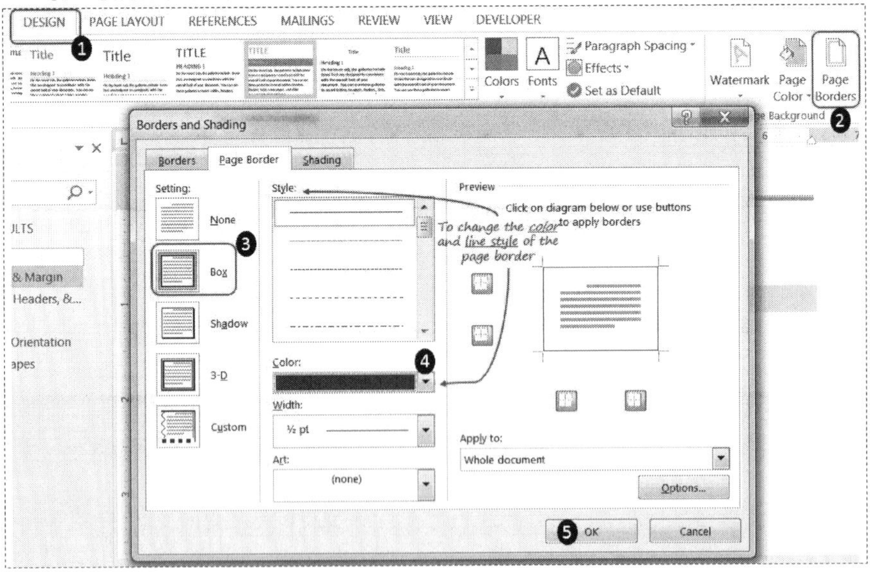

A page border should now be applied to the **PresentationAndGraphics** file

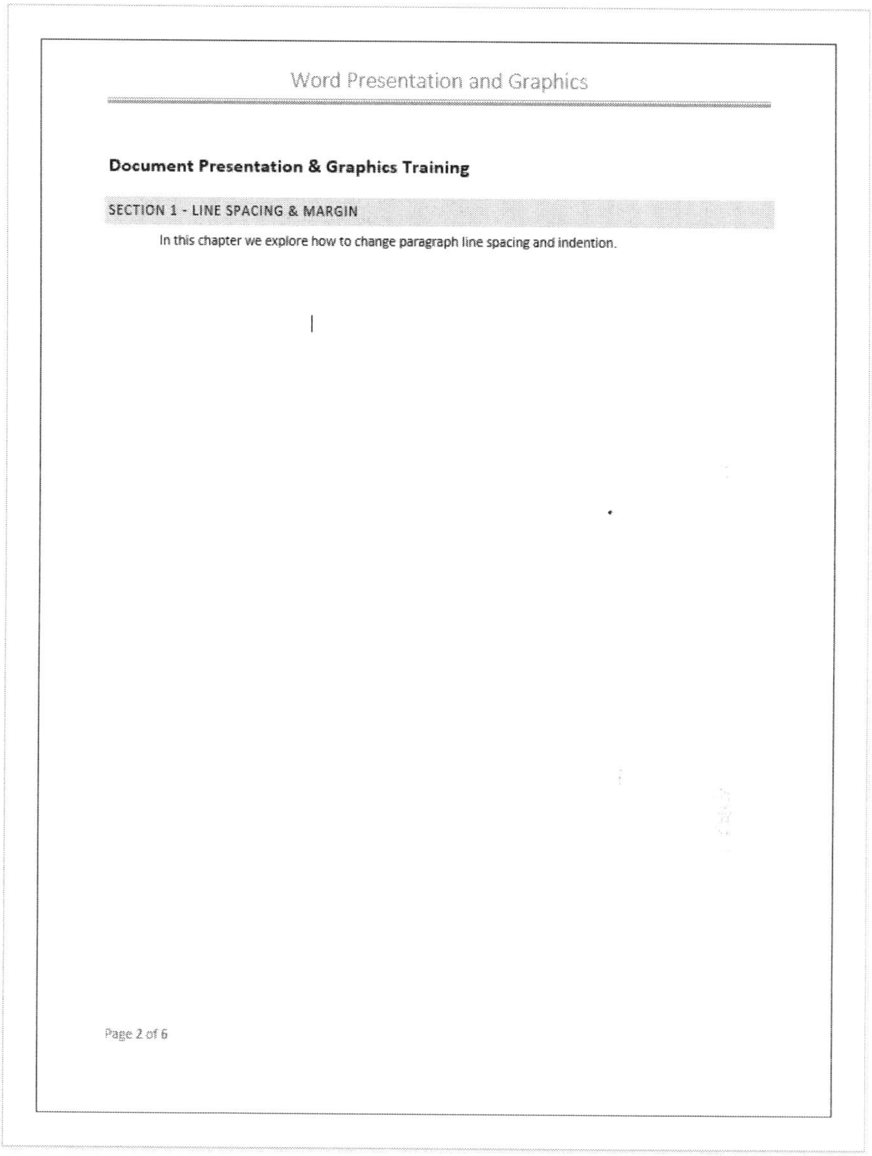
Word Presentation and Graphics
Document Presentation & Graphics Training
SECTION 1 - LINE SPACING & MARGIN
In this chapter we explore how to change paragraph line spacing and indention.
Page 2 of 6

6. **Save** the **PresentationAndGraphics.docx** file

CHAPTER 14

Spellcheck & Thesaurus

Functionality:

- **Spellcheck**: is a default feature within Microsoft® Word® that identifies misspelled words. Microsoft® Word® will also attempt provide the correct spelling of the word.
- **Thesaurus**: an optional utility, when evoked provides a list words that are synonyms of a selected word.

Spellcheck

The Spellcheck and AutoCorrect features within Microsoft® Word® are normally active when you start Microsoft® Word®.

1. If you mistype a word, a jagged red line will appear underneath the incorrect spelling
2. Right-click over the misspelled word and if Microsoft® Word® has a corrected suggested spelling, it will appear in a pop-up menu
3. Click the correct spelling of the word

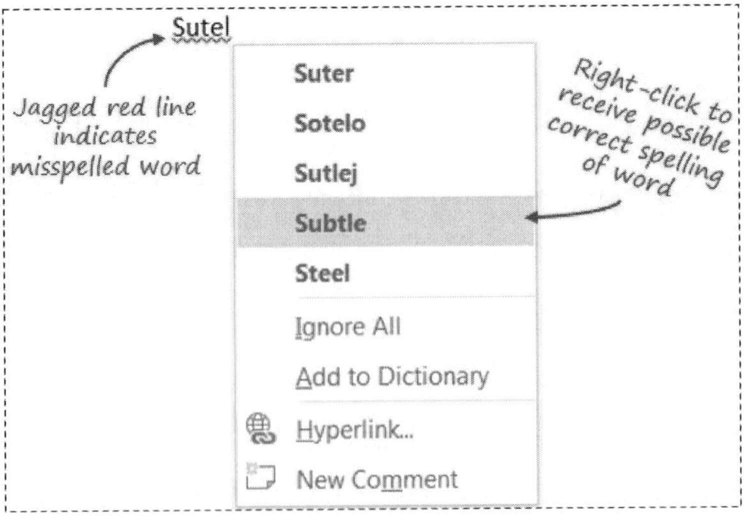

Custom Dictionaries

You may also add words to a Custom Dictionary such as a company name or abbreviation.

1. Right-click over the company name or abbreviation
2. From the pop-up menu, select **'Add to Dictionary'**

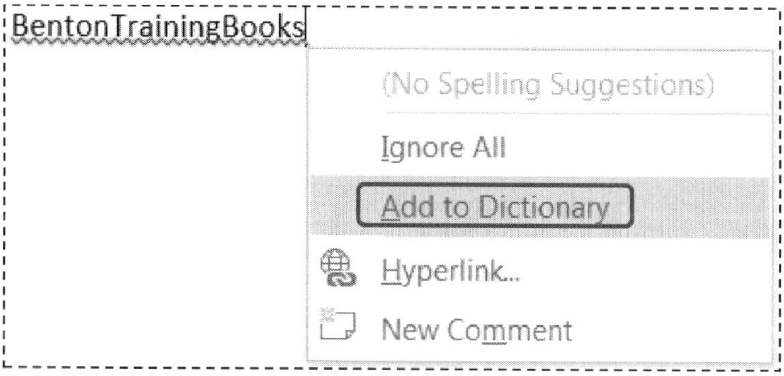

To edit the words in your Custom Dictionary

3. From the Ribbon, select **File : Options : Proofing**
4. Under the section *'When correcting spelling in Microsoft Office programs'*, click the **'Custom Dictionaries…'** button

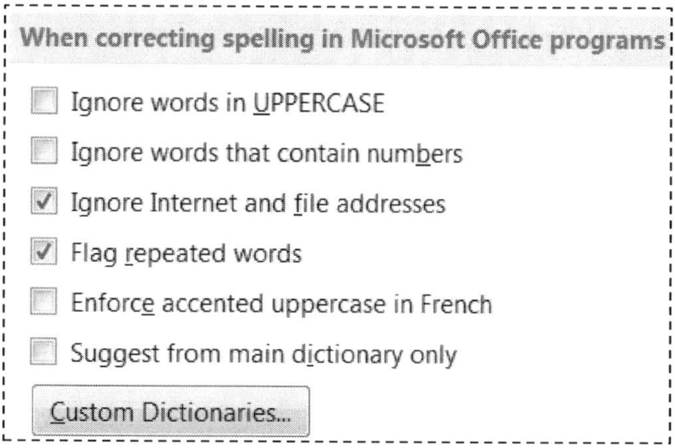

Thesaurus

It is not uncommon when you have a large document to inadvertently over use a particular word. This is where having a built-in thesaurus is quite helpful.

1. Highlight the word you would like to replace with something similar
2. Using your keyboard, press **'Shift+F7'** *or* from the Ribbon, select the **'REVIEW'** tab and click the **Thesaurus icon**

On the left-hand side of your screen will appear a listing of possible similar words.

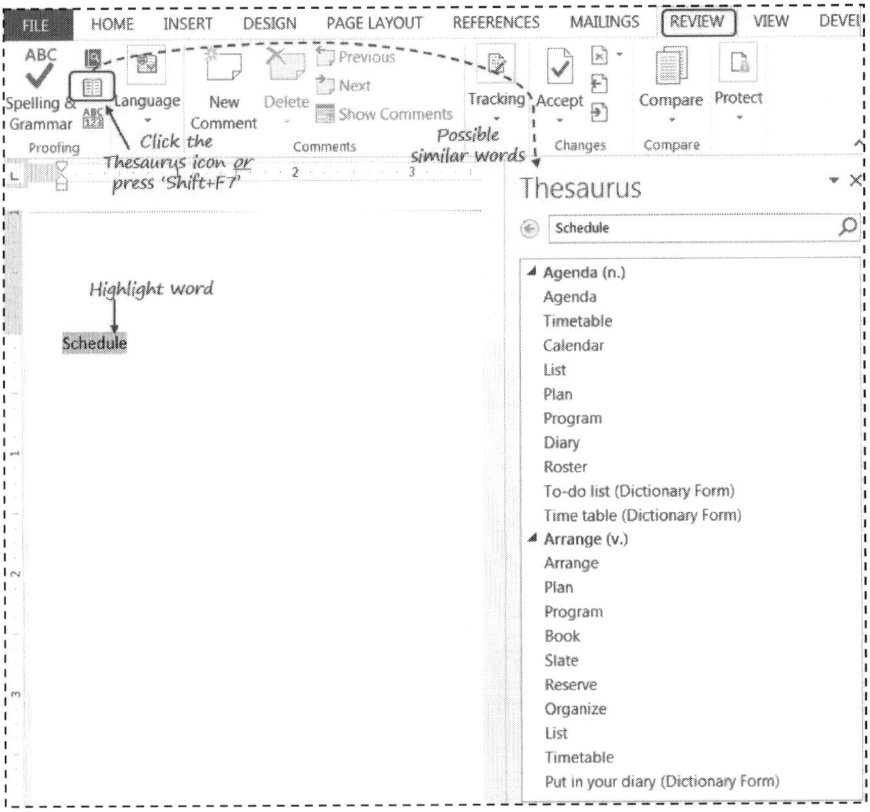

CHAPTER 15

Find, Replace, & Go-To

Functionality:

- **<u>Find</u>**: locates specific content in a document
- **<u>Replace</u>**: replaces content you have identified, such as words or characters with other material
- **<u>Go-To</u>:** Use to quickly navigate to a specific area of the document, such as a Page number, Section, Line, or Bookmark

---

<u>EXAMPLES:</u>

Find

1. From the Ribbon select the **HOME** tab
2. Click the 

button or on your keyboard press shortcut keys **CTRL + F**
3. The **'Navigation Pane'** will appear, enter the word you're searching for
4. Select the **'RESULTS'** section to see all the entries found

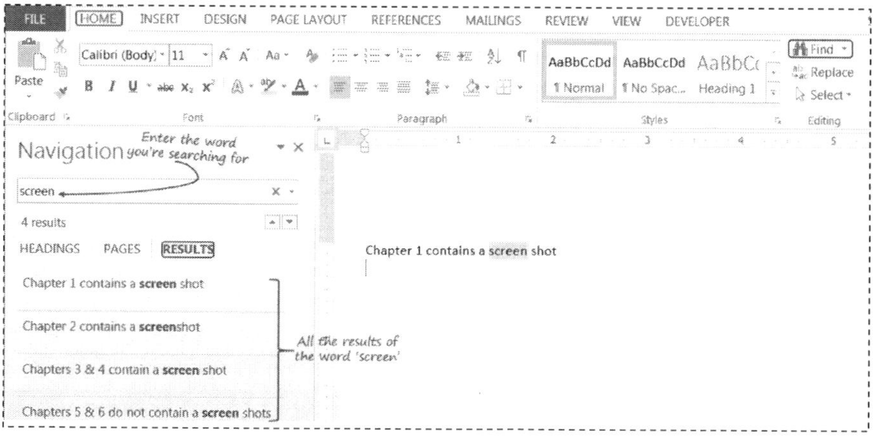

Replace

1. From the Ribbon select the **HOME** tab
2. Click the  button or on your keyboard press shortcut keys **CTRL + H**
3. The **'Find and Replace'** dialogue box will appear, enter:
   - The word you want to *REPLACE* in the **'Find what:'** box
   - The word you want to *REPLACE WITH* in the **'Replace with:'** box
4. Click the appropriate option:
   - **Replace** = replaces each matching entry one-by-one
   - **Replace All** = replaces ALL matches

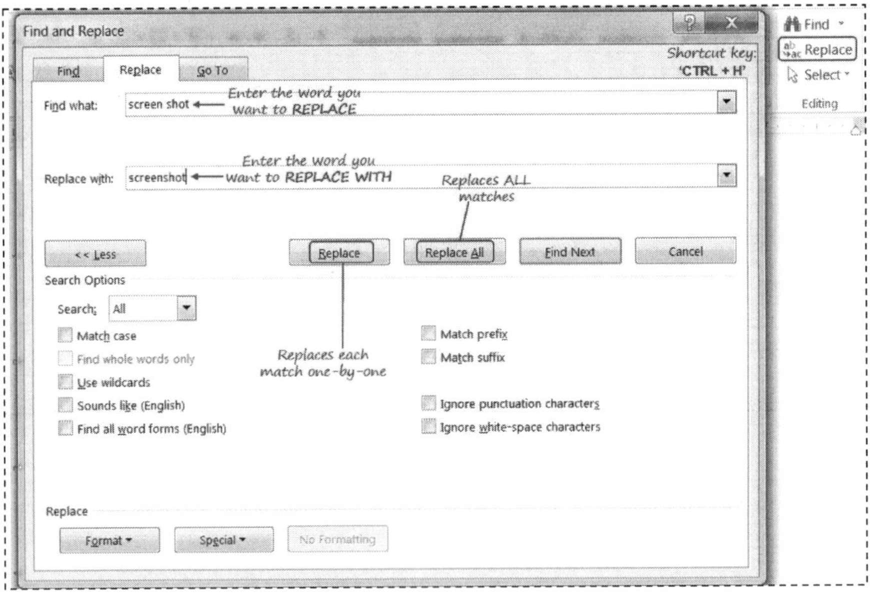

Go-To

1. From the Ribbon select the **HOME** tab
2. Click the  button or on your keyboard press shortcut keys **CTRL + G**

3. The **'Find and Replace**' dialogue box will appear, select the **'Go To'** tab
4. Under the '**Go to what:'** section select the appropriate option, such as *Page, Section, Line, Bookmark etc.*
5. Enter the page number or other option
6. Click the **'Go To'** button

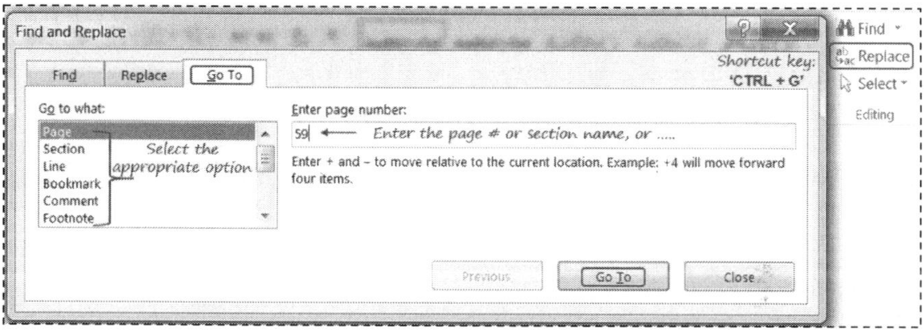

CHAPTER 16

Track Changes & Document Compare

Functionality:

- **Track Changes**: The Track Changes feature allows you to review edits to a document made by other users. You may accept or reject all or some of these alterations.
- **Document Compare**: This feature will compare two documents and display the differences between them in a *third document.*
  - The two compared documents DO NOT need to be the same name, however should be similar versions of each other.
  - The original two compared documents are not changed, during the compare process.
  - You may accept or reject all or some of the differences between two compared documents and 'Save As' a new third document.

EXAMPLES:

Track Changes

1. Open the file we created in Chapter 6 named: **PresentationAndGraphics.docx**
2. Go-To page 2
3. From the Ribbon select the **REVIEW** tab and either:
   - Click the drop-down box for **'Track Changes'** and select **'Track Changes'** *or*
   - From the bottom of your screen, click the **'TRACK CHANGES: OFF'** toggle field

Please see image on next page:

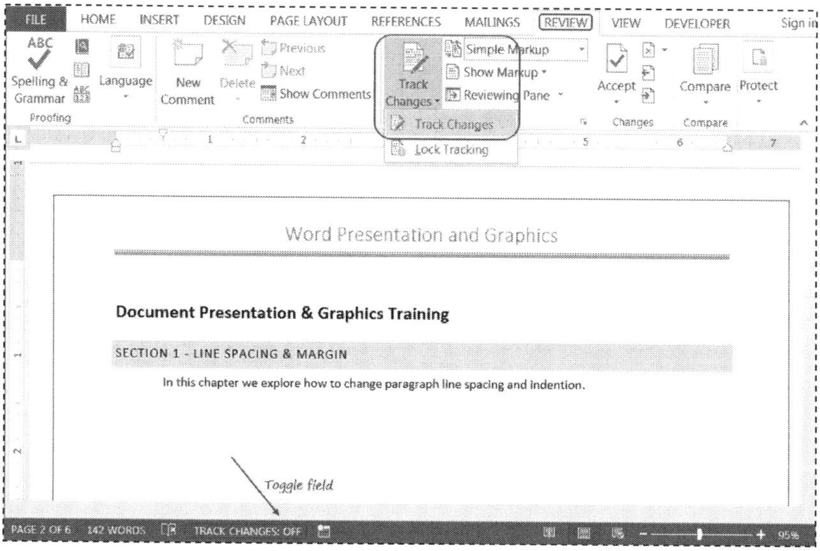

4. Delete the word **'chapter'** and replace with the word **'section'** in the line: *'In this chapter we explore how to…'*

5. Under the **'Reviewing Pane'** drop-down box select **'Reviewing Pane Vertical…'**

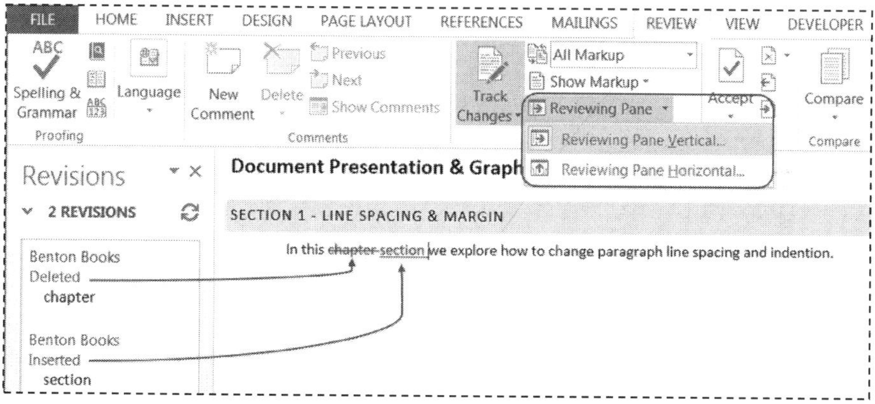

6. Accept the changes by either:
   - Clicking the **'Accept'** button *or*
   - Right-clicking and selecting **'Accept Insertion'**

Please see image on next page:

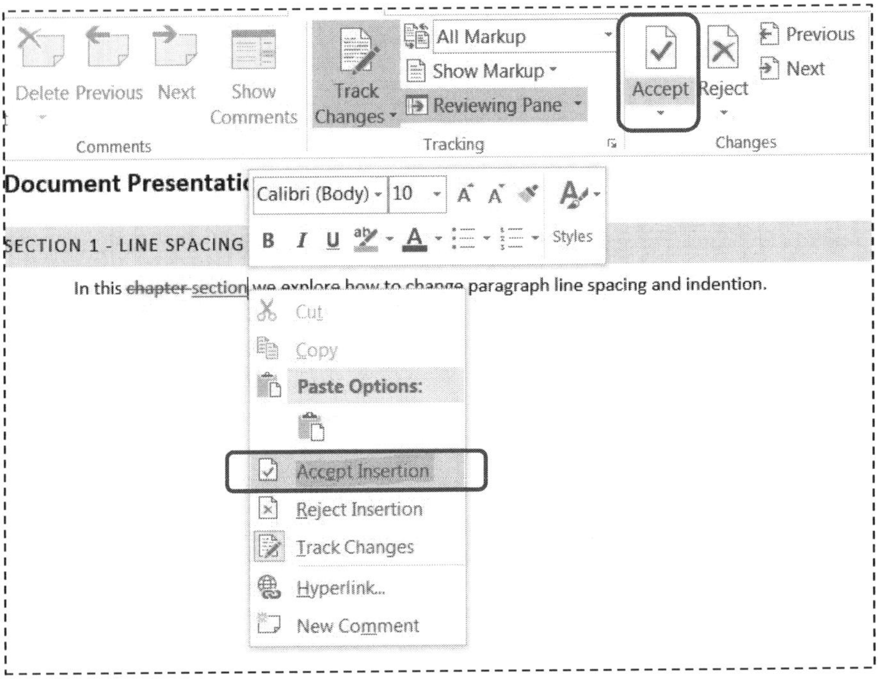

7. Turn off Track Changes by either:
   - Click the **'Track Changes'** icon on the **REVIEW** tab *or*
   - From the bottom of your screen, click the **'TRACK CHANGES: ON'** toggle field
8. **Save** the **PresentationAndGraphics.docx** file

Compare Two Version Of Similar Documents

Using the compare feature within Microsoft® Word® is helpful when comparing versions of documents created at different times or by different users *AND Track Changes was not used.*

The following is **not an exercise,** but does explain how the process works when comparing two similar versions of documents:

- From the Ribbon you would select the **REVIEW** tab and **'Compare…'** from the **'Compare'** drop-down box

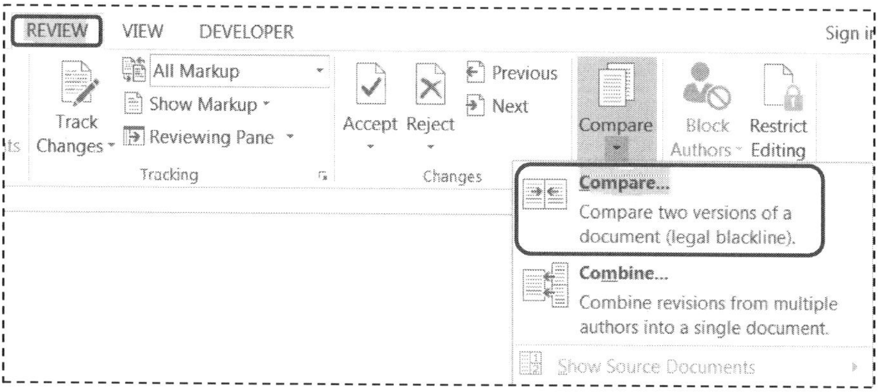

The following dialogue box will appear:

- In the **'Original document'** drop-down box you would select the document that you want to use as the primary document
- In the **'Revised document** drop-down box you would select document you want to compare
- Then click the **'OK'** button

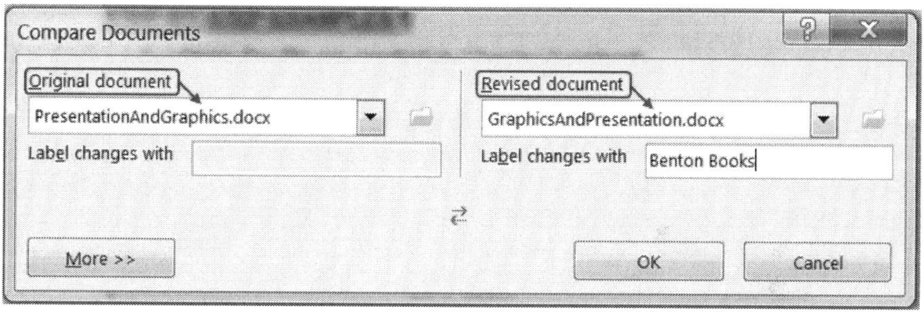

- A **new compare document** will be created

Please see image on next page:

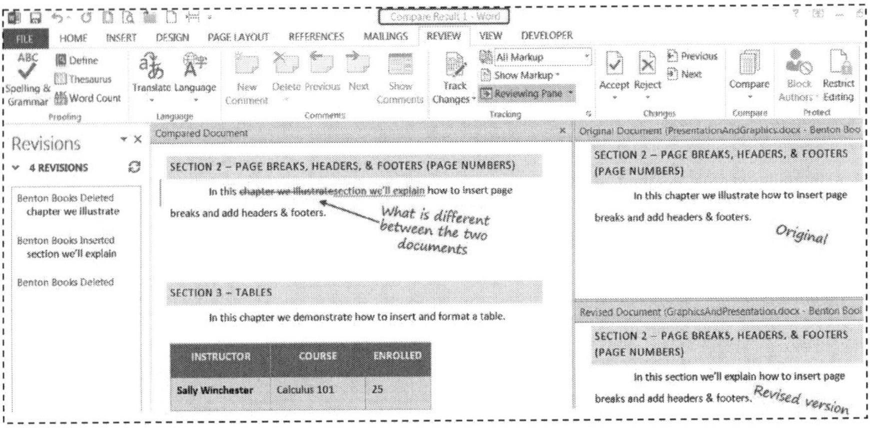

- After reviewing the differences, you may accept or reject all or some of the changes between the two compared documents.
- Then **'Save As'** the combined new document

CHAPTER 17

Read-Only & Password Protected Documents

In the last chapter we reviewed methods to track changes and compare versions of similar documents, however there may be times when you do not wish to have your document modified. The two most common approaches to preventing alterations are:

1. Setting the document properties to **Read-Only**
2. Password protecting the document

STEP-BY-STEP EXAMPLES:

Read-Only

1. Open the file we created in Chapter 6 named: **PresentationAndGraphics.docx**
2. From the Ribbon, select the **'File'** tab
3. Click the menu option **'Save As'**
4. Select the **C:\WordTraining** folder
5. Click the **'Tools'** drop-dox and select **'General Options…'**

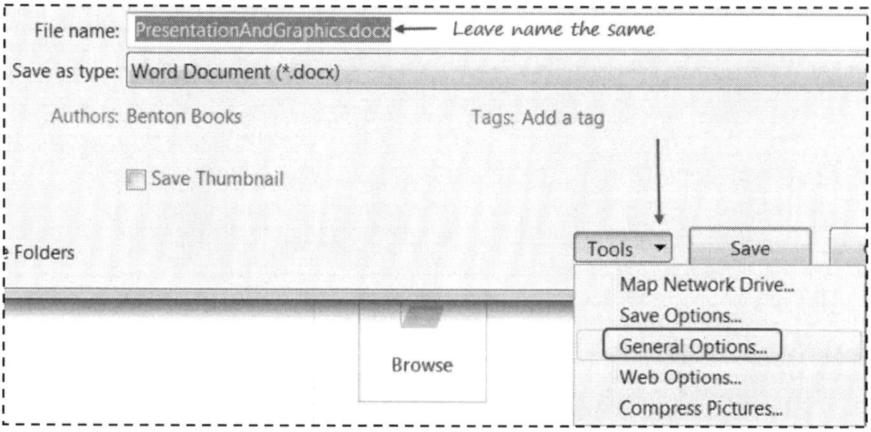

6. In the **'Password to modify:'** box enter **test**
7. Click the check box for **'Read-only recommended'**
8. Click the **'OK'** button

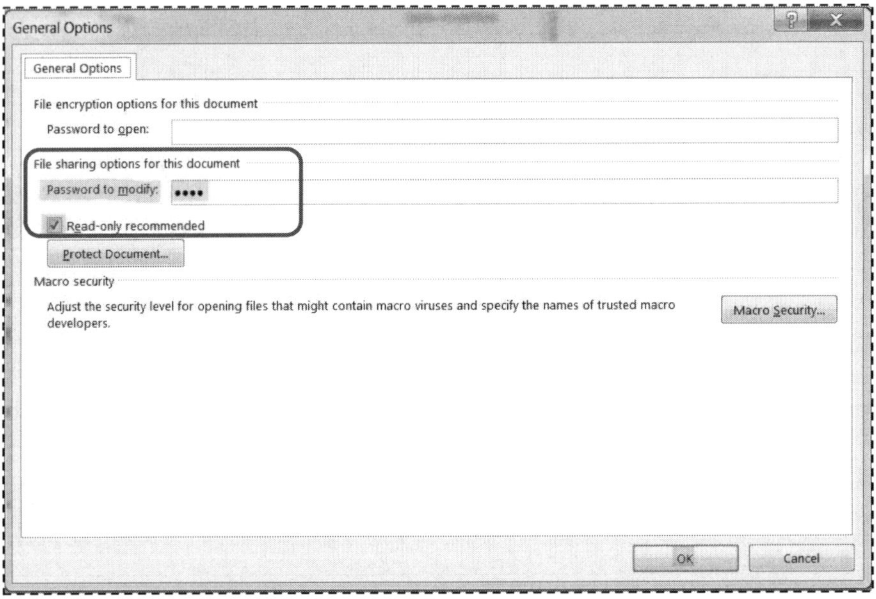

9. Click the **'Save'** button
10. Close and re-open the file
11. At the prompt click the **'Read-Only'** button, the user would need to enter the correct password in order to modify

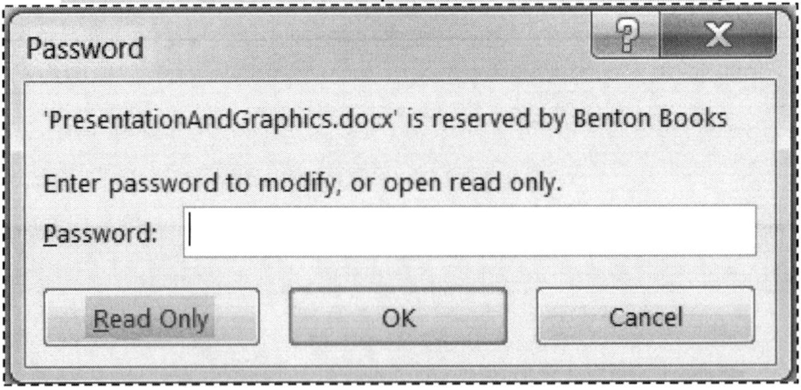

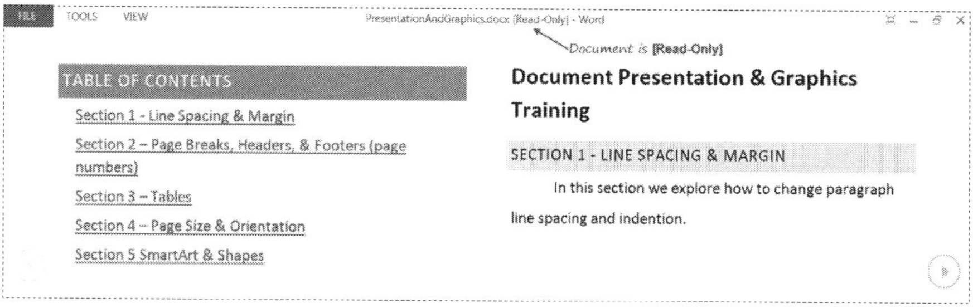

12. From the Ribbon, select the **'File'** tab and **'Close'**

Password Protecting Files

1. Re-open the **PresentationAndGraphics.docx** file
2. At the prompt, enter the password **test**
3. From the Ribbon, select the **'File'** tab
4. Click the menu option **'Save As'**
5. Select the **C:\WordTraining** folder
6. Click the '**Tools'** drop-dox and select **'General Options…'**
7. In the **'Password to open:'** box enter **test**
8. Click the check box for **'Read-only recommended'**
9. Click the **'OK'** button

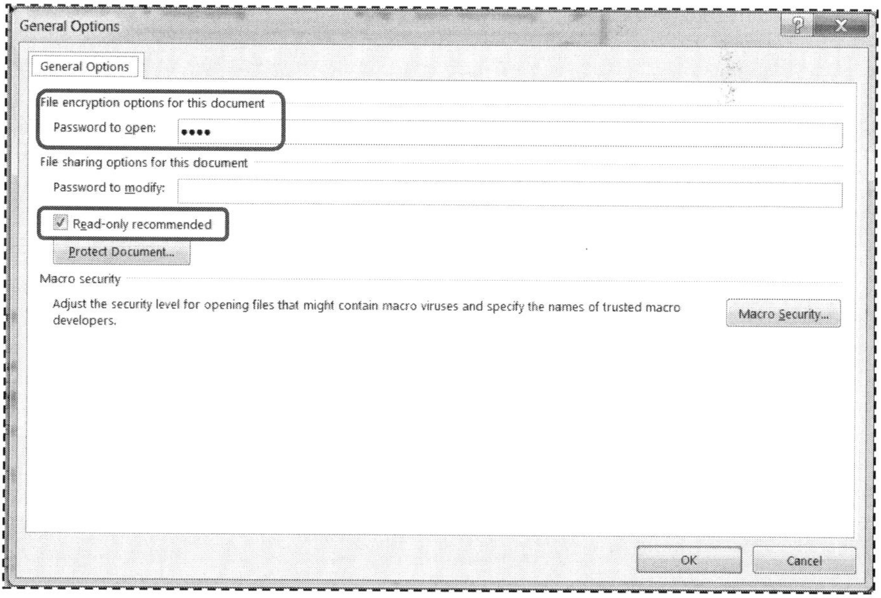

10. At the **'Confirm Password'** prompt, re-enter **test**
11. Click the **'OK'** button

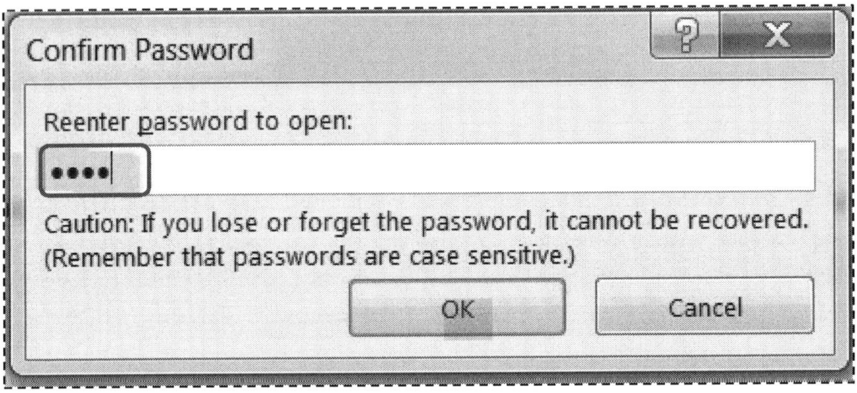

12. Click the **'Save'** button
13. Close and re-open the file

Unless the correct password is provided, the user will not be able to open the file:

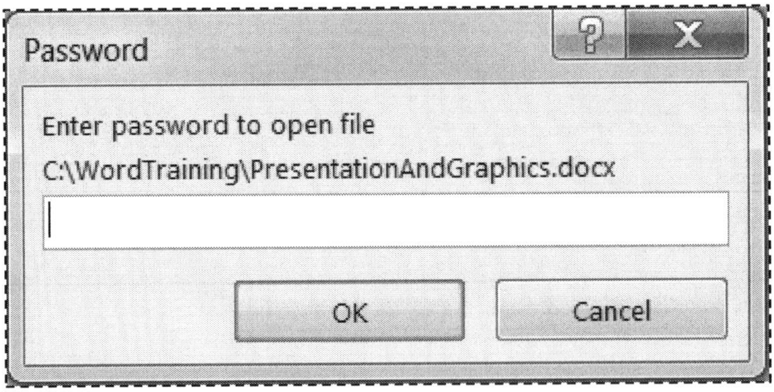

CHAPTER 18

Watermarks - classify documents as 'Confidential' or as a 'Draft'

Watermarks are useful as they convey the *condition of a document* such as a ***work-in-progress*** or ***draft*** by displaying these words on each page of the file. If the word ***confidential*** is used, it may help to reduce unauthorized sharing of sensitive or restricted information.

An additional benefit, is watermarks can also support brand familiarity by incorporating a ***company logo*** on a sales receipt, purchase order, or other organizational materials.

EXAMPLE:

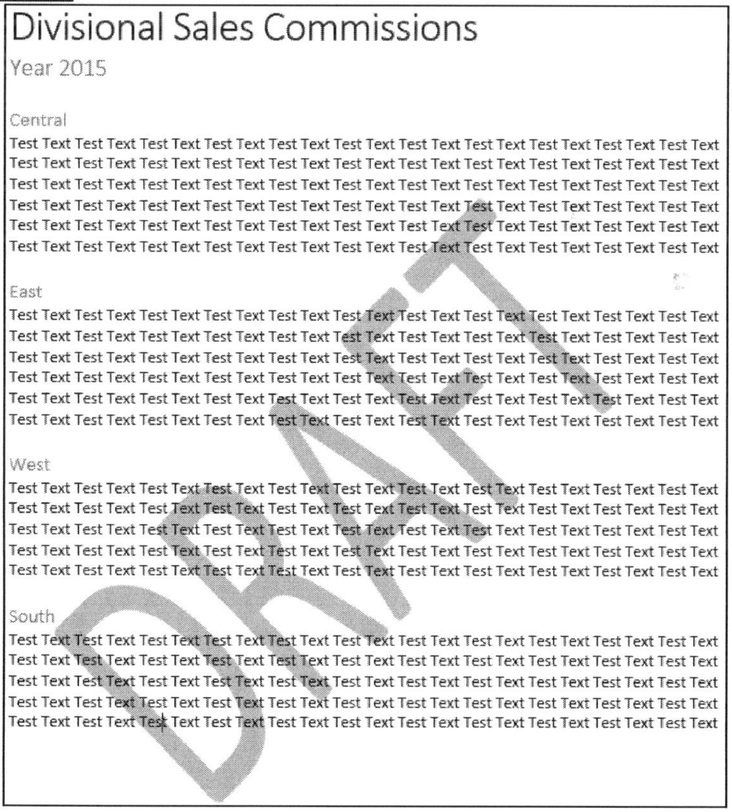

Divisional Sales Commissions

Year 2015

Central

Test Text Test Text Test Text Test Text Test Text Test Text Test Text Test Text Test Text Test Text Test Text
Test Text Test Text Test Text Test Text Test Text Test Text Test Text Test Text Test Text Test Text Test Text
Test Text Test Text Test Text Test Text Test Text Test Text Test Text Test Text Test Text Test Text Test Text
Test Text Test Text Test Text Test Text Test Text Test Text Test Text Test Text Test Text Test Text Test Text
Test Text Test Text Test Text Test Text Test Text Test Text Test Text Test Text Test Text Test Text Test Text
Test Text Test Text Test Text Test Text Test Text Test Text Test Text Test Text Test Text Test Text Test Text

East

Test Text Test Text Test Text Test Text Test Text Test Text Test Text Test Text Test Text Test Text Test Text
Test Text Test Text Test Text Test Text Test Text Test Text Test Text Test Text Test Text Test Text Test Text
Test Text Test Text Test Text Test Text Test Text Test Text Test Text Test Text Test Text Test Text Test Text
Test Text Test Text Test Text Test Text Test Text Test Text Test Text Test Text Test Text Test Text Test Text
Test Text Test Text Test Text Test Text Test Text Test Text Test Text Test Text Test Text Test Text Test Text
Test Text Test Text Test Text Test Text Test Text Test Text Test Text Test Text Test Text Test Text Test Text

West

Test Text Test Text Test Text Test Text Test Text Test Text Test Text Test Text Test Text Test Text Test Text
Test Text Test Text Test Text Test Text Test Text Test Text Test Text Test Text Test Text Test Text Test Text
Test Text Test Text Test Text Test Text Test Text Test Text Test Text Test Text Test Text Test Text Test Text
Test Text Test Text Test Text Test Text Test Text Test Text Test Text Test Text Test Text Test Text Test Text
Test Text Test Text Test Text Test Text Test Text Test Text Test Text Test Text Test Text Test Text Test Text

South

Test Text Test Text Test Text Test Text Test Text Test Text Test Text Test Text Test Text Test Text Test Text
Test Text Test Text Test Text Test Text Test Text Test Text Test Text Test Text Test Text Test Text Test Text
Test Text Test Text Test Text Test Text Test Text Test Text Test Text Test Text Test Text Test Text Test Text
Test Text Test Text Test Text Test Text Test Text Test Text Test Text Test Text Test Text Test Text Test Text
Test Text Test Text Test Text Test Text Test Text Test Text Test Text Test Text Test Text Test Text Test Text

DRAFT

STEP-BY-STEP EXAMPLE:

1. Open Microsoft® Word® and create a new blank Word® document – **(shortcut keys CTRL + N)**

2. Type and format the following lines of text:
   - **Example How To Use Watermarks**
   - Watermark example using the word 'DRAFT'

3. From the Ribbon select the **DESIGN** tab, and click the drop-down list for **'Watermark'**

4. Scroll-down to the to the **'Disclaimers'** section and select **'DRAFT 1'**

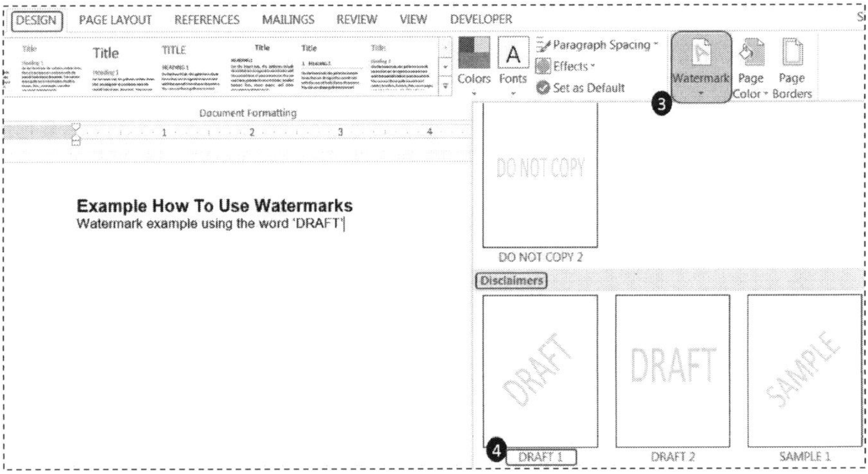

The word **'DRAFT'** should now appear diagonally across the document.

5. To change the *text or formatting* of the watermark, from the Ribbon select the tab **DESIGN**

6. Click the '**Watermark'** drop-down button and select **'Custom Watermark…'**

Please see image on next page:

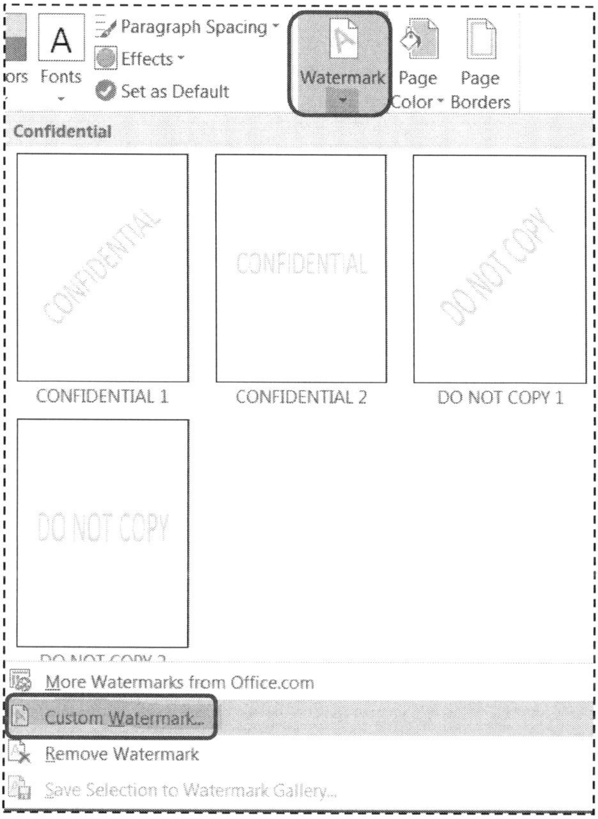

The following dialogue box will appear:

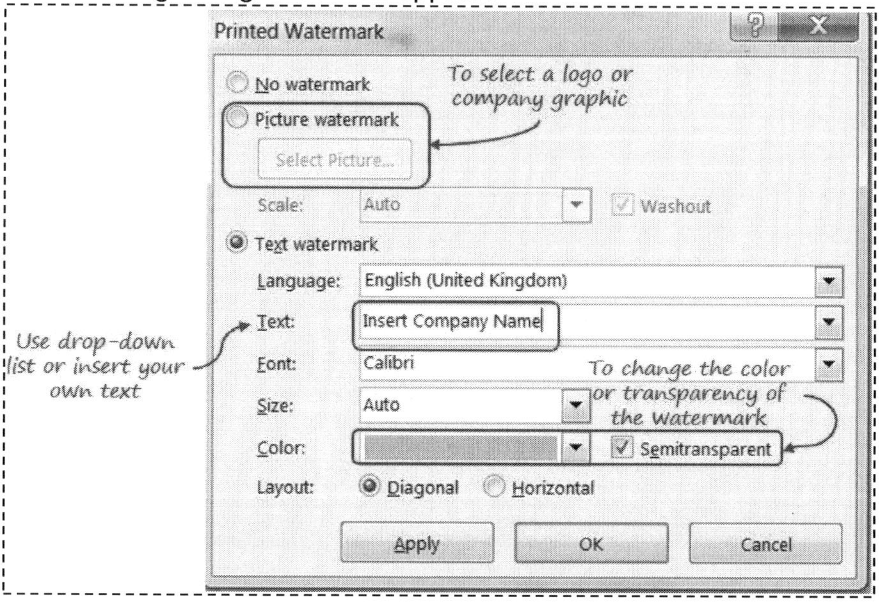

Removing a Watermark

- To remove a watermark, from the Ribbon select the tab **DESIGN**
- Click the **'Watermark'** drop-down button and select **'Remove Watermark'**

CHAPTER 19

Mail Merge Process Overview

What is Mail Merge?

Mail Merge is a feature within Microsoft® Word® that allows you to create mass communications in which specific sections can be tailored to individuals or groups. Examples include:

- Letters *(i.e. to customers or employees)*
- Advertisements, Promotional, or Marketing Materials
- Invoices
- Emails *(i.e. to customers or employees)*
- Mailing Labels

One of the main benefits of Mail Merge is you're able to take advantage of existing lists of customer or employee data, and can customize the communication medium without having to manually change each correspondence. The Mail Merge feature saves time and reduces the chance of errors occurring when someone must physically type or modify each message.

Since Mail Merge is part of the Microsoft® Office® product suite, it interfaces with other Microsoft® Office® products such as:

- Microsoft® Access®
- Microsoft® Excel®
- Microsoft® Outlook®

This association provides the ability to maintain customer or employee data separately and adapt each communication with minimal effort.

What are the main parts of Mail Merge?

All Mail Merge communication consists of three parts:

1. **Data Source:** The Data Source contains the individual information to customize the communication. Items such as customer or employee data.
2. **Document Type:** The Document Type contains *both* the fields that are to be merged *(individualized information)* as well as the text that does not change. Document Types include *Documents (i.e. letters, invoices, recipes etc.)*, *Emails*, *Mailing Labels*, or *Envelopes*.
3. **Merged Document**: The Merged Document is the *output of merge*. For example, the personalized finished Letter, Label, or Email tailored for each recipient.

Conceptual diagram of the Mail Merge process:

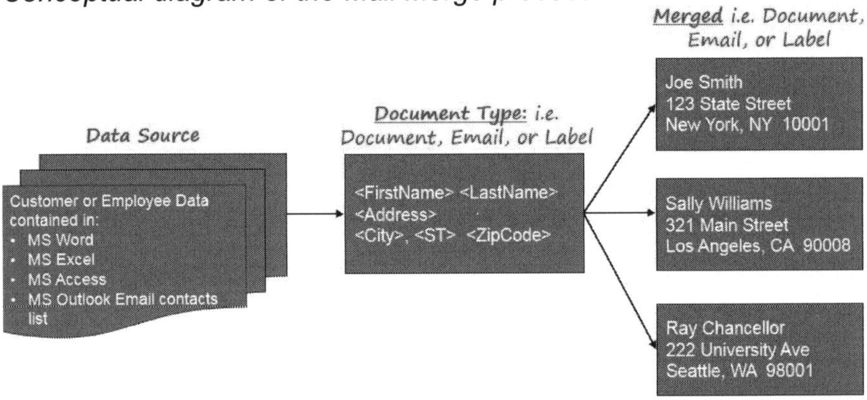

CHAPTER 20

Mail Merge - Form Letters

For our first example using the Mail Merge feature we'll create a form letter to communicate an upcoming employee event.

The following will guide you through the basic Mail Merge functionality, including how to *setup a Data Source file*, *creating the letter*, and *viewing the merged letters before printing*.

Creating The Data Source File

STEP-BY-STEP EXAMPLE:

1. Open Microsoft® Word® and create a new blank Word® document **(CTRL + N)**
2. From the Ribbon select **INSERT : TABLE** 7 columns and 4 rows

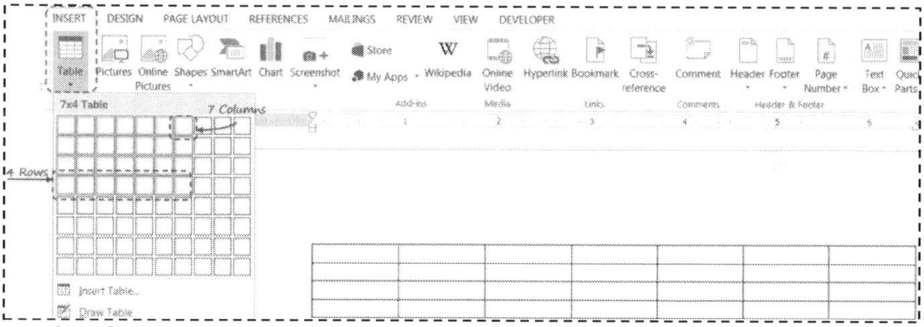

3. Create a new folder called: **C:\MailMergeTraining**
   - Open **Windows Explorer** *(see chapter 3, page 16)*
   - Select the folder **C:** and click **'New Folder'**

4. Name the newly created folder: **MailMergeTraining**
5. Save the Word® data source file **(CTRL + S)** name it **MailMergeDataSource.docx** in the newly created folder

6. Enter the following headings in the first row of the table:
    - FirstName *(make sure no space between First & Name)*
    - LastName *(make sure no space between Last & Name)*
    - Address
    - City
    - ST
    - ZipCode *(make sure no space between Zip & Code)*
    - DOB *(Date Of Birth)*

FirstName	LastName	Address	City	ST	ZipCode	DOB

Add the source data:

FirstName	LastName	Address	City	ST	ZipCode	DOB
Joe	Smith	123 State Street	New York	NY	10001	05/01/1975
Sally	Williams	321 Main Street	Los Angeles	CA	90008	11/18/1985
Ray	Chancellor	222 University Ave	Seattle	WA	98001	02/25/1969

7. Enter the following under **FirstName**:
    - Joe
    - Sally
    - Ray
8. Enter the following under **LastName**:
    - Smith
    - Williams
    - Chancellor
9. Enter the following under **Address**:
    - 123 State Street
    - 321 Main Street
    - 222 University Ave
10. Enter the following under **City**:
    - New York
    - Los Angeles
    - Seattle
11. Enter the following under **ST**:
    - NY
    - CA
    - WA

12. Enter the following under **ZipCode**:
    - 10001
    - 90008
    - 98001
13. Enter the following under **DOB**:
    - 05/01/1975
    - 11/18/1985
    - 02/25/1969
14. **Save (CTRL + S)** and **Close** the file

Creating The Letter Document

1. Create a new blank Word® document **(CTRL + N)**
2. Type the following text information:

19 September 2016

Dear :

Open Enrollment begins **01 October 2016** through **31 October 2016**. To change your elections, logon via the company benefits website and enter the following information:

```
First Name:
 Last Name:
   Address:
       DOB:
```

Thank you,
HR Department

3. **Save** the form letter to: **C:\MailMergeTraining**
4. Name the letter: **FormLetter.docx**

5. From the Ribbon select **MAILINGS : Start Mail Merge : Step-by-Step Mail Merge Wizard…**

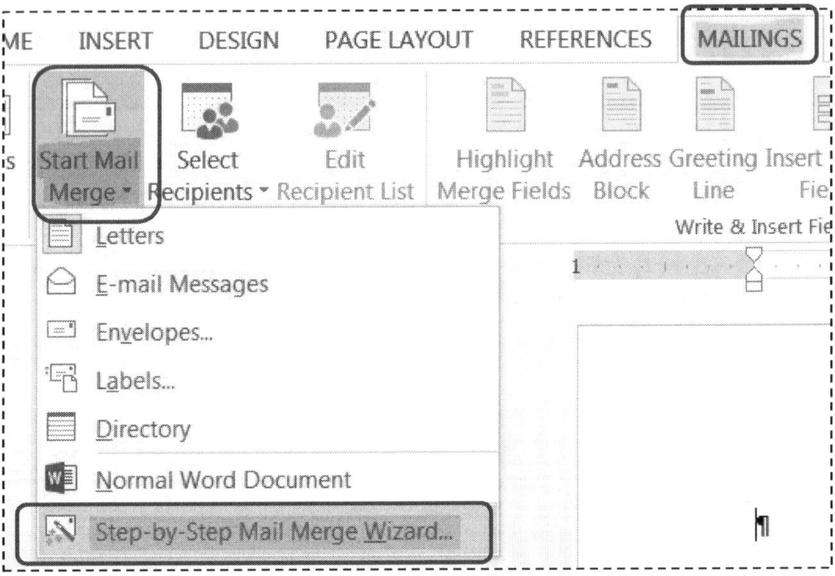

The following wizard should now appear on your screen

6. Under **'Select document type'** verify the **'Letters'** radio button is selected

7. Click **'Next: Starting document'**

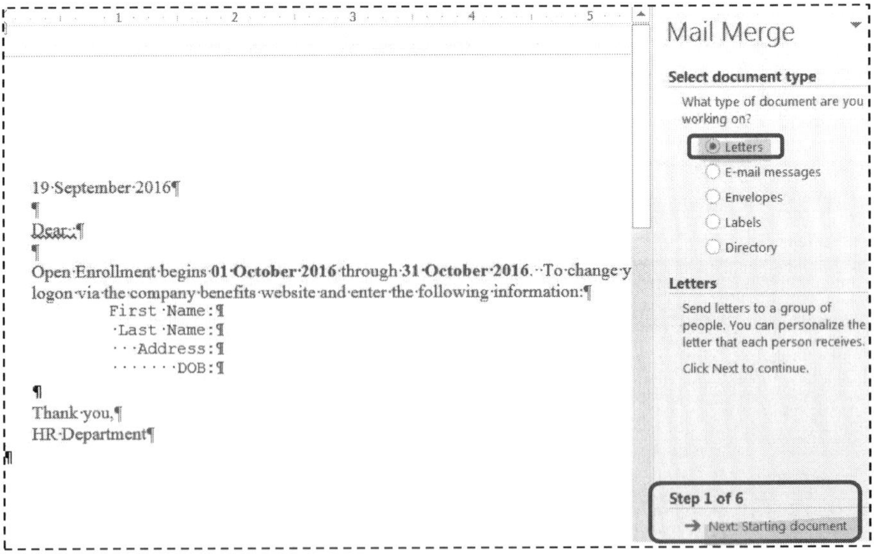

8. Click **'Next: Select recipients'**

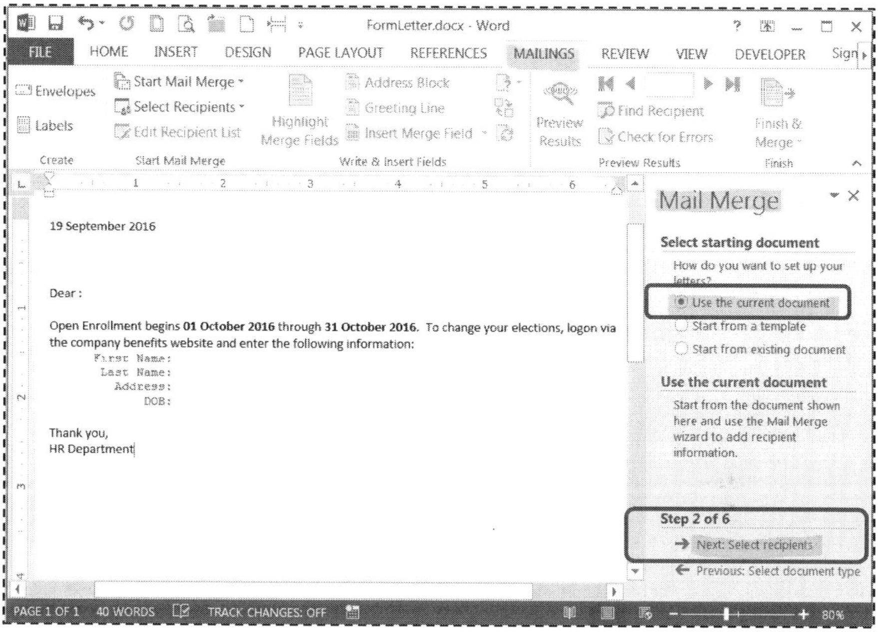

9. Under **'Use an existing list',** click the **'Browse…'** option

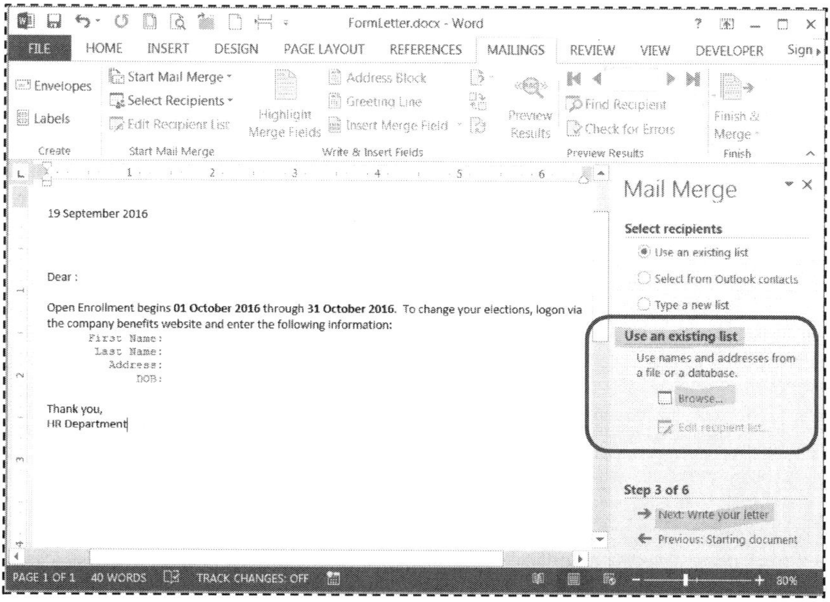

10. When prompted, open the **C:\MailMergeTraining** folder

11. Select the file: **'MailMergeDataSource.docx'**

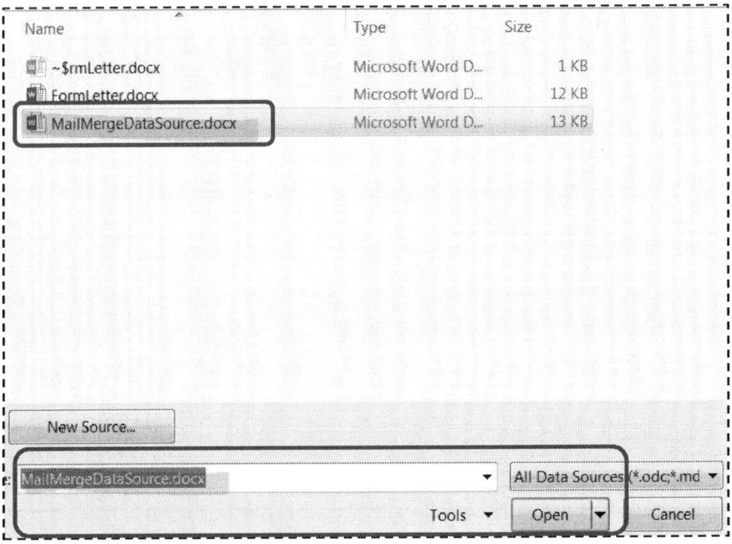

12. Click the **'Open'** button

The following prompt will appear:

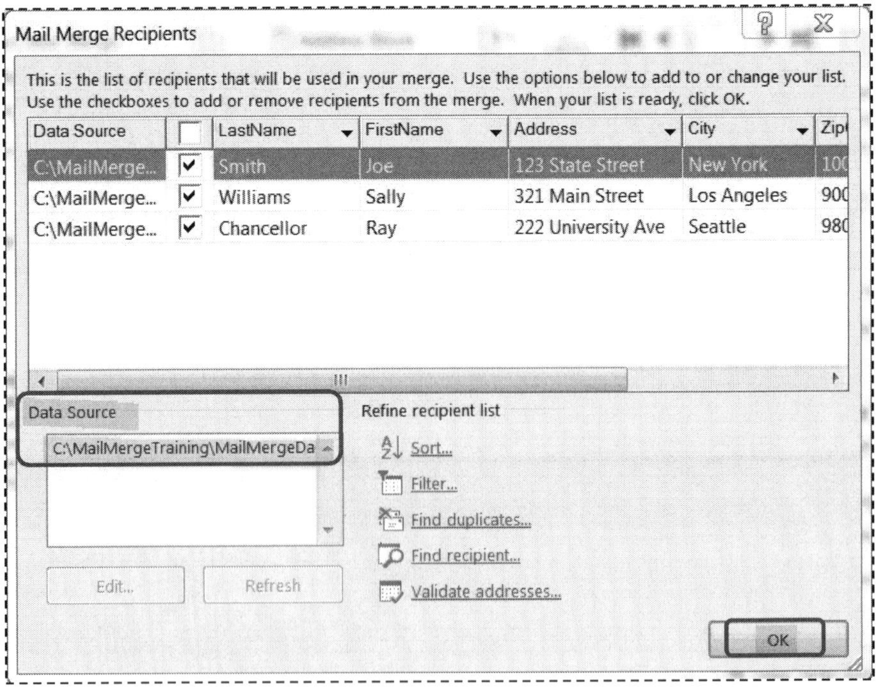

13. Click the **'OK'** button

14. Place your cursor in front of the word **'Dear'**

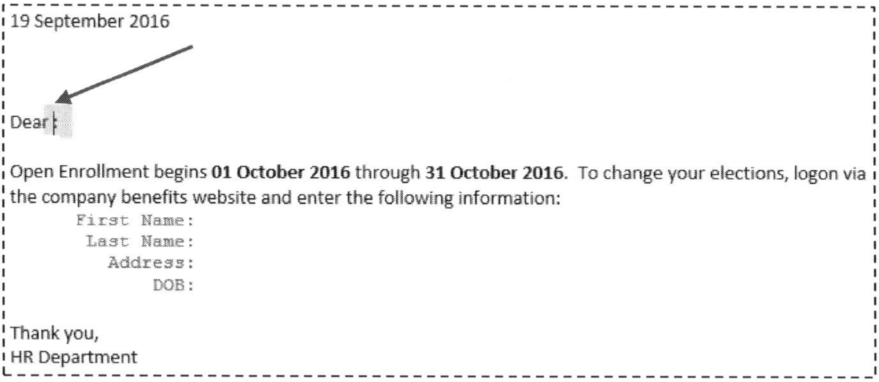
19 September 2016

Dear :

Open Enrollment begins **01 October 2016** through **31 October 2016**. To change your elections, logon via the company benefits website and enter the following information:

First Name:
Last Name:
Address:
DOB:

Thank you,
HR Department

15. From the **'MAILINGS'** tab select the **'Insert Merge Field'** drop-down box
16. Select **'FirstName'** *(should be inserted after the word 'Dear')*
17. After **'FirstName'** press your **'Spacebar'** on your keyboard

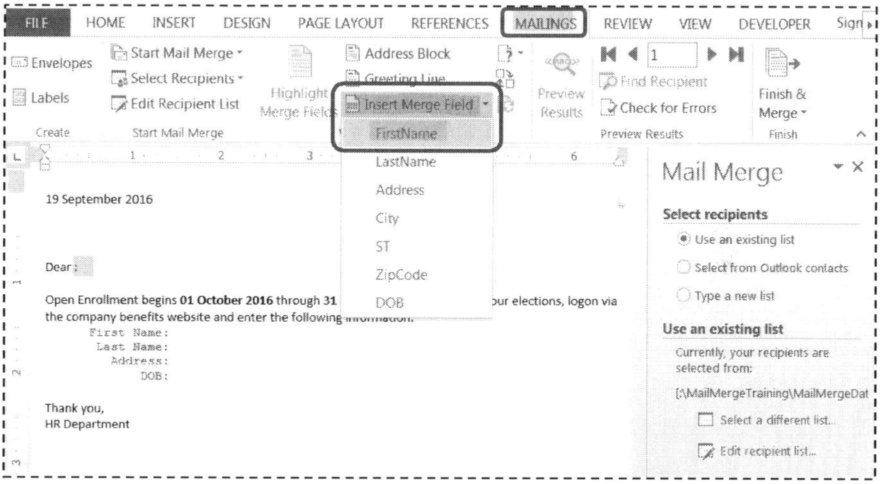

18. From the **'Insert Merge Field'** drop-down box Select **'LastName'** *(should be inserted after FirstName and space)*

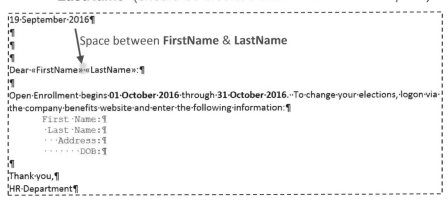

19·September·2016¶
¶
¶ Space between **FirstName** & **LastName**
¶
Dear·«FirstName»·«LastName»:¶
¶
Open·Enrollment·begins·**01·October·2016**·through·**31·October·2016**.··To·change·your·elections,·logon·via·the·company·benefits·website·and·enter·the·following·information:¶
First·Name:¶
·Last·Name:¶
···Address:¶
·······DOB:¶
¶
Thank·you,¶
HR·Department¶

19. Place your cursor after the words `First Name:`
20. Add a space *(press the spacebar on your keyboard)*
21. From the **'Insert Merge Field'** drop-down box select **'FirstName'**
22. Repeats steps 19 - 21 for fields:
    - Last Name: «LastName»
    - Address: «Address»
    - DOB: «DOB»

The **'FormLetter'** document should look similar to the following:

19 September 2016

Dear «FirstName» «LastName»:

Open Enrollment begins **01 October 2016** through **31 October 2016**. To change your elections, logon via the company benefits website and enter the following information:
First Name: «FirstName»
Last Name: «LastName»
Address: «Address»
DOB: «DOB»

Thank you,
HR Department

23. **Save** the file **(CTRL + S)**

The SQL Prompt (opening a document containing merged fields)

After saving and closing a document that contains merged fields, and then re-opening that file, you're *linking* to a data source, Microsoft® refers to this as "database." As such, when opening a document that contains merged fields you'll receive the following prompt, simply **click 'Yes'**, to proceed with opening the document.

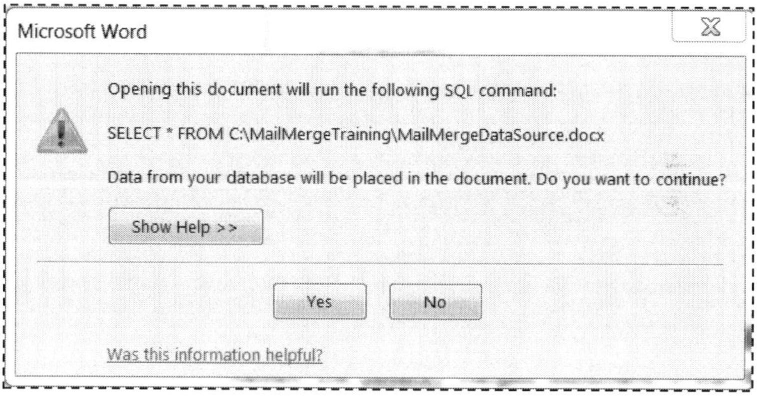

Merging The Document

1. With the **'FormLetter'** document open, select the **'MAILINGS'** tab
2. Select the **'Finish & Merge'** drop-down box and then **'Edit Individual Documents…'**

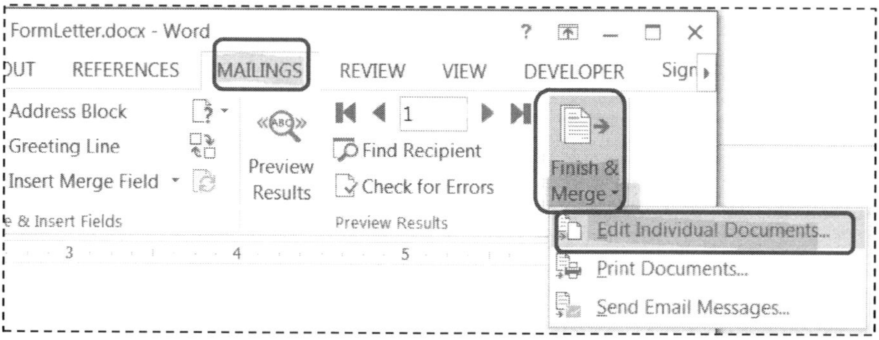

The following prompt should appear:

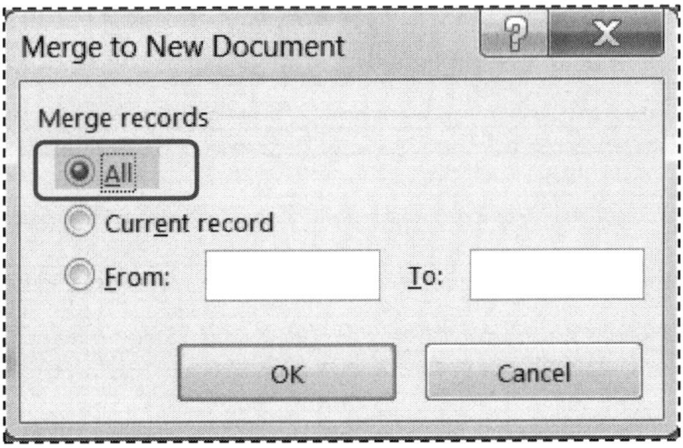

3. If not already selected, select the **'All'** radio button
4. Click the **'OK'** button

A new Word document should now be created, note the personalized information:

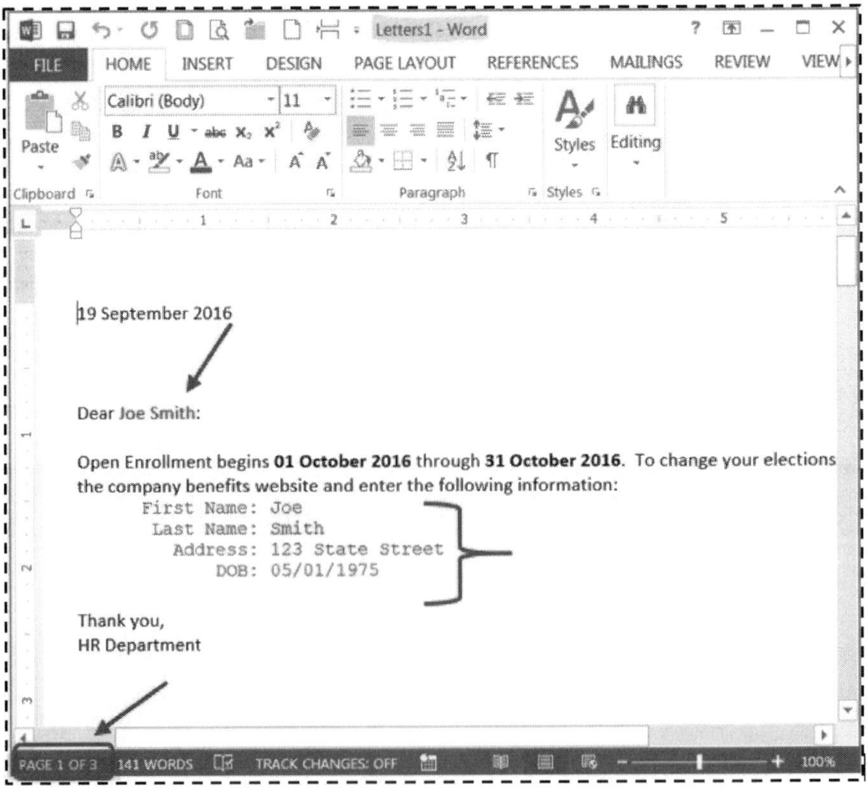

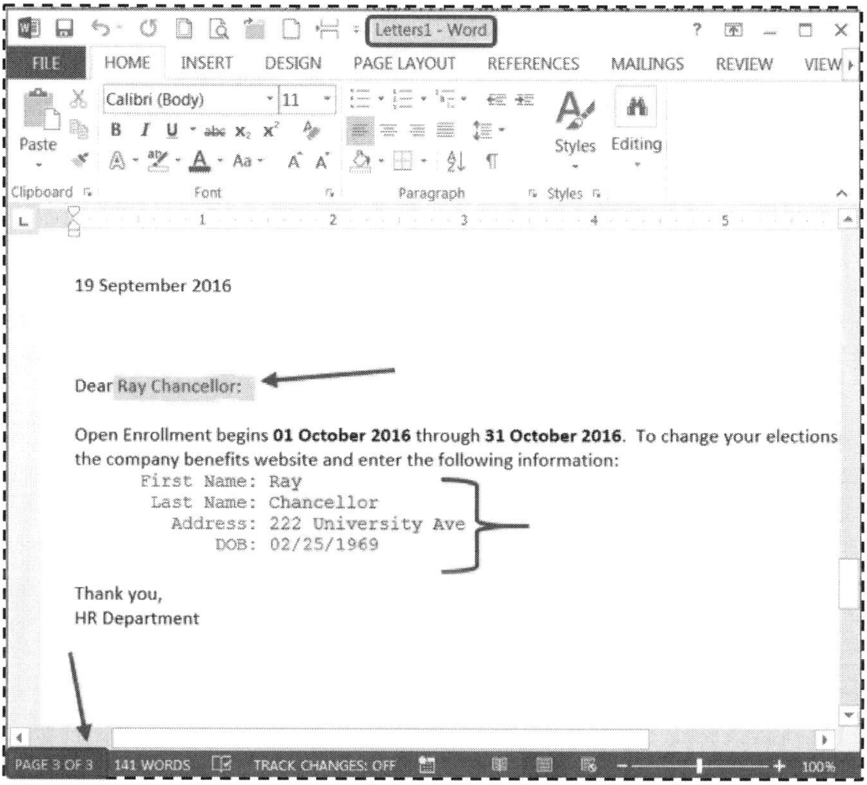

Review the **'Letters1'** merged document, if the results are as you expected them to be, you may *rename and save* the file or *print out* each letter for distribution.

Helpful Tips

To easily see your document's merged fields, click the button **'Highlight Merge Fields'**. This will highlight each merged field.

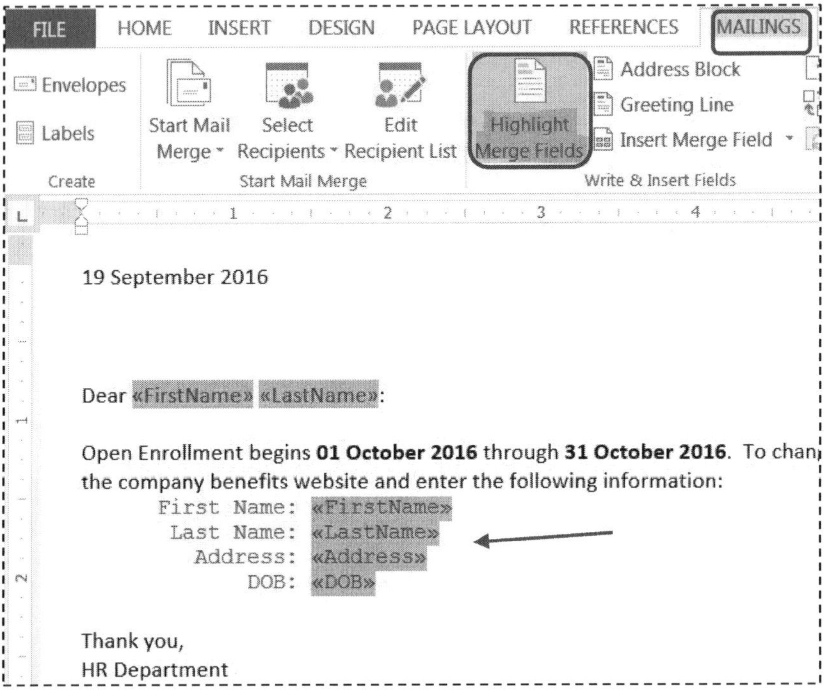

Before generating the merged document, you may preview the merged records, by clicking the button **'Preview Results'**. This is especially useful if you're incorporating many merge fields or generating a large number of merged records.

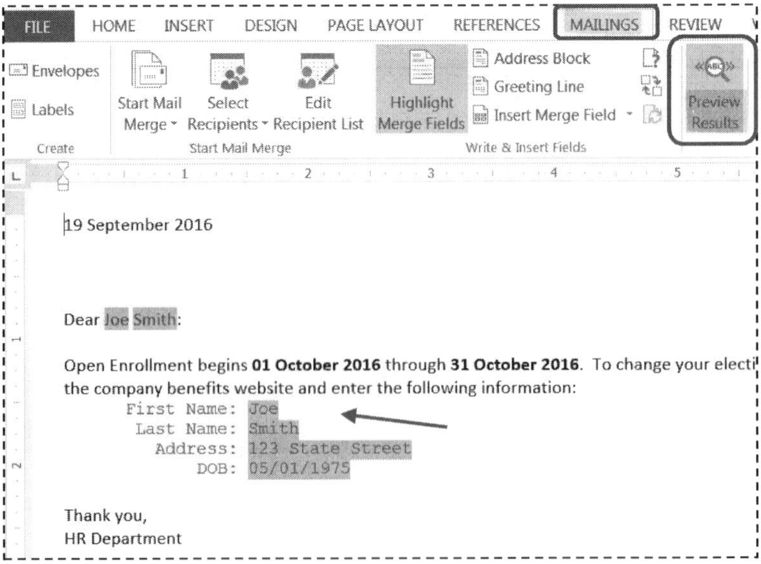

CHAPTER 21

Mail Merge - Mailing Labels

In this chapter we learn how to create mailing labels. To save time we'll use the existing Data Source file created in chapter 20.

You may complete this exercise even if you don't have labels for printing.

STEP-BY-STEP EXAMPLE:

Creating The Label Document

1. Open Microsoft® Word® and create a new blank Word® document **(CTRL + N)**
2. From the Ribbon select **MAILINGS : Start Mail Merge : Step-by-Step Mail Merge Wizard…**

The following wizard should now appear on your screen

3. Under **'Select document type'**, choose the **'Labels'** radio button
4. Click **'Next: Starting document'**

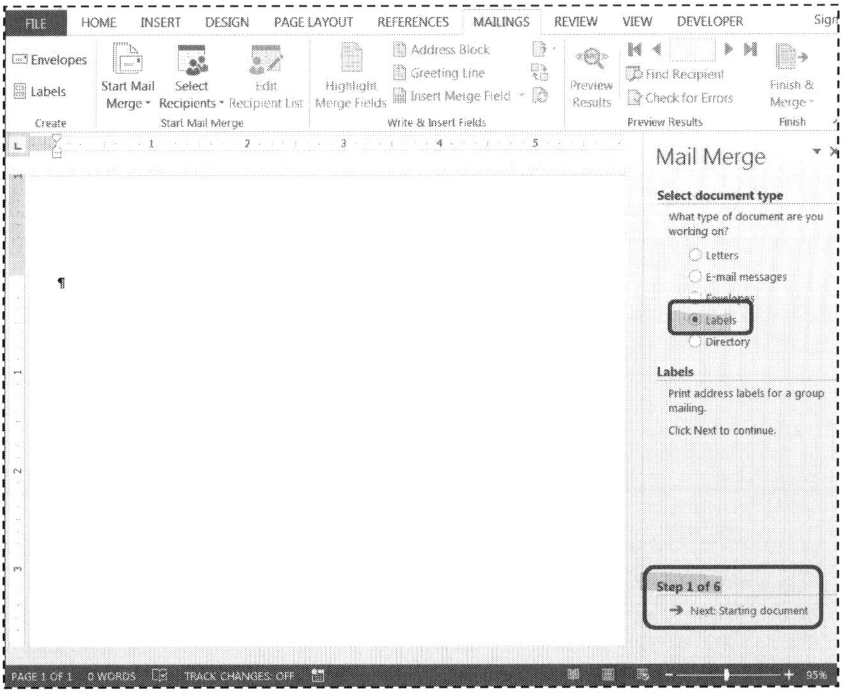

5. Under **'Change document layout'** select **'Label options…'**

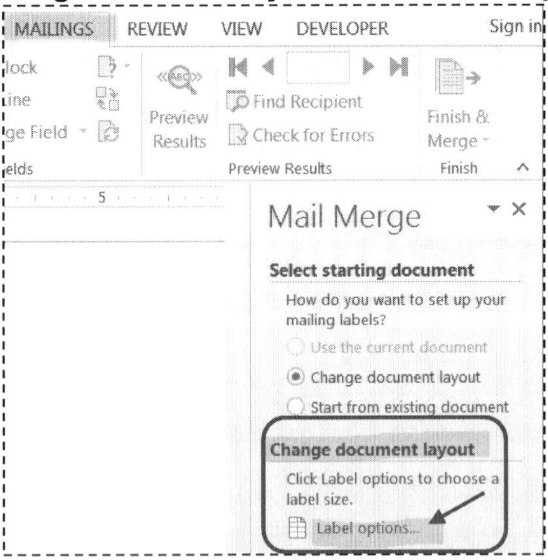

6. Choose the appropriate label option for your country and product number. ***You may complete this exercise even if you don't have labels for printing.***
7. Click the **'OK'** button
8. Click **'Next: Select recipients'**

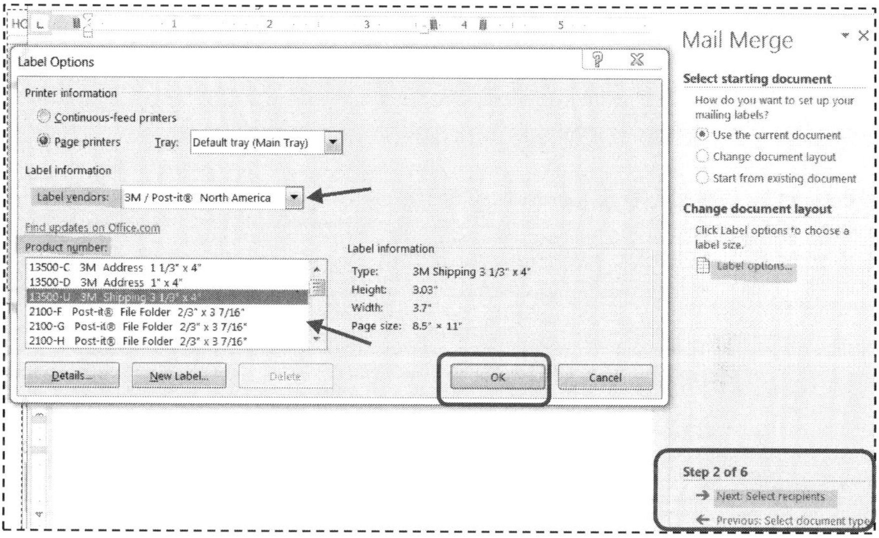

9. Under **'Use an existing list',** click the **'Browse…'** option

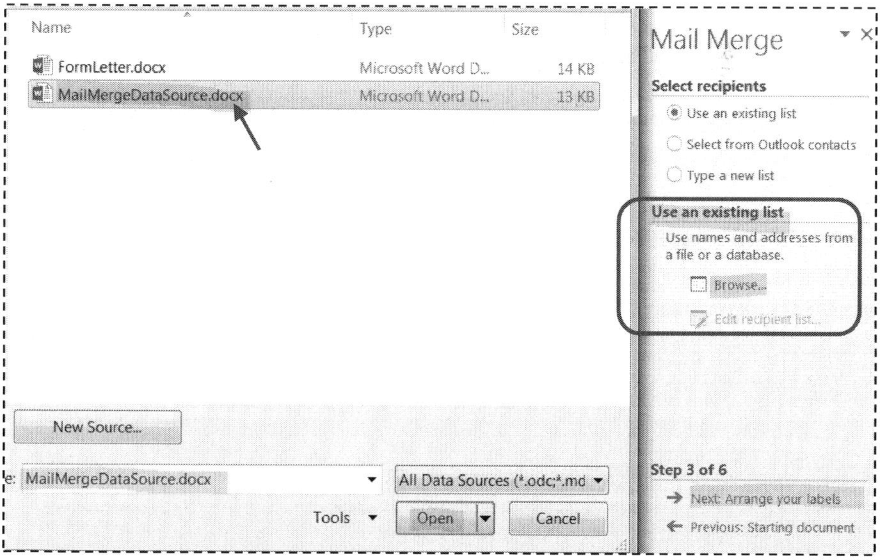

10. When prompted, open the **C:\MailMergeTraining** folder

11. Select the file: **'MailMergeDataSource.docx'**
12. Click the **'Open'** button

The following prompt will appear:

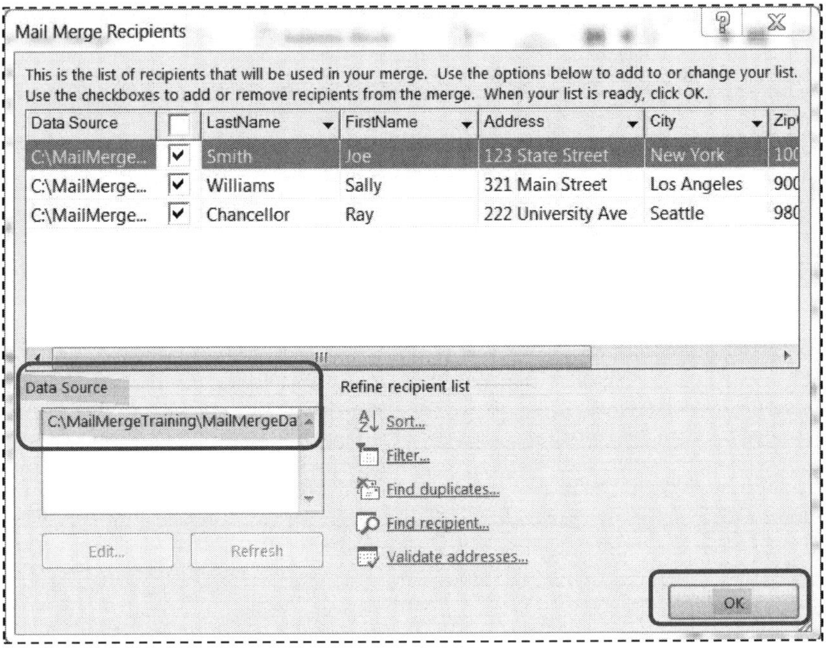

13. Click the **'OK'** button

You should now see a result *similar* to the following:

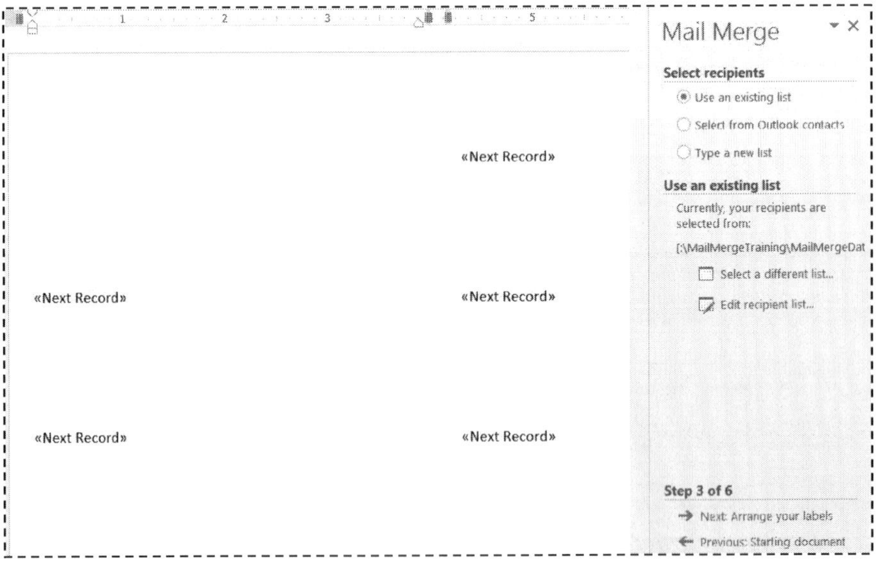

14. To assist with readability, from the Ribbon select **TABLE TOOLS : DESIGN**
15. Using the **'Borders'** drop-down box select **'View Gridlines'**

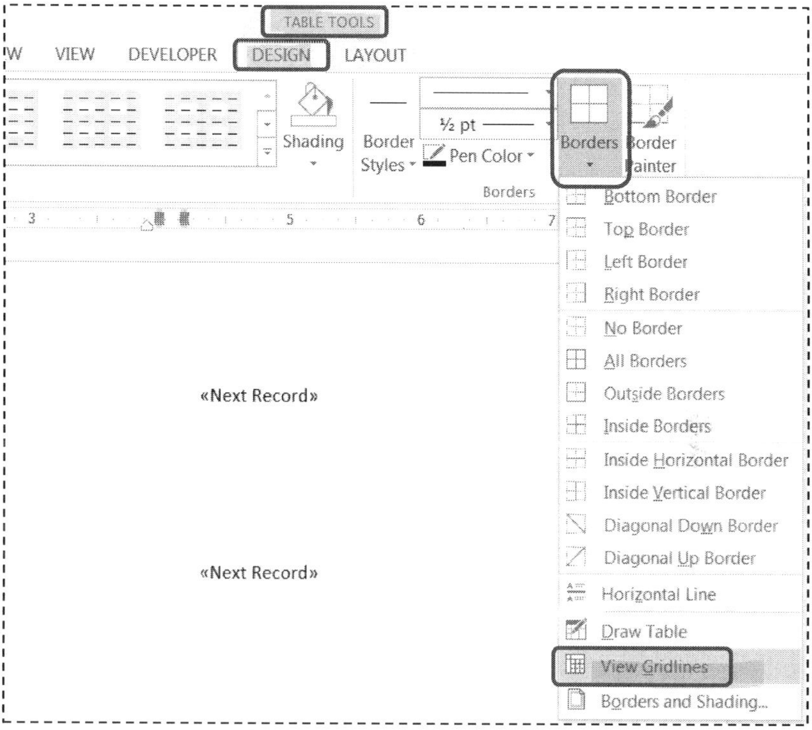

16. Place your cursor in the first label box

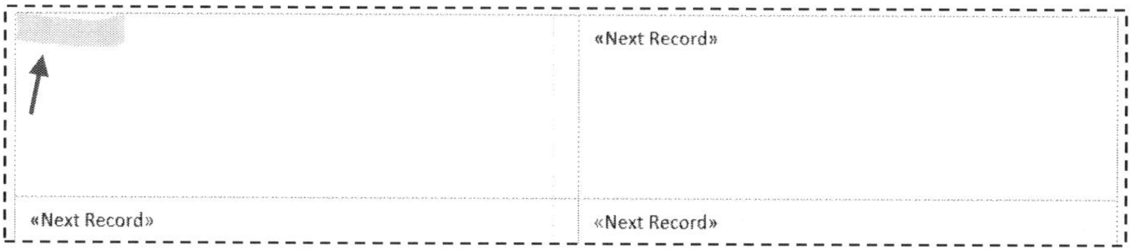

17. From the **'MAILINGS'** tab select the **'Insert Merge Field'** drop-down box, select **'FirstName'**
18. After **'FirstName'** press your **'Spacebar'** on your keyboard

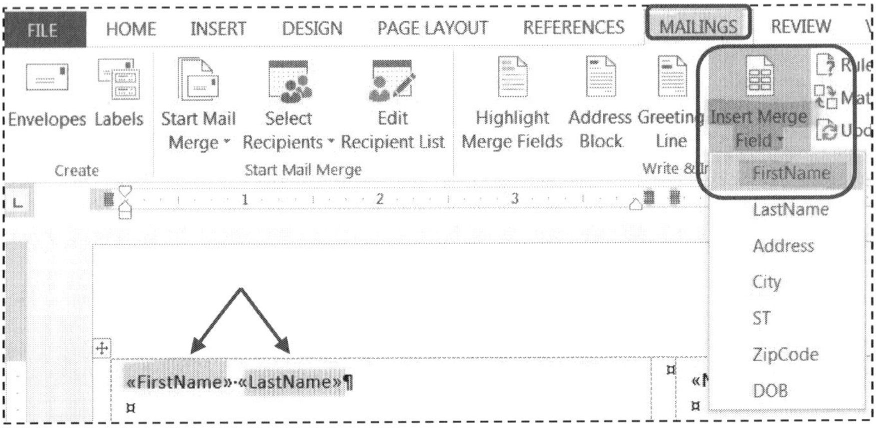

19. From the **'Insert Merge Field'** drop-down box select **'LastName'** *(should be inserted after FirstName and space)*
20. On a new line, under «FirstName» «LastName» select the **'Insert Merge Field'** drop-down box and **'Address'**
21. On a new line, under «Address» select the **'Insert Merge Field'** drop-down box and **'City'**
22. After **'City'** insert a comma (,) and press your **'Spacebar'** on your keyboard
23. From the **'Insert Merge Field'** drop-down box select **'ST'** *(should be inserted after City, and space)*
24. After **'ST'** press your **'Spacebar'** on your keyboard twice
25. From the **'Insert Merge Field'** drop-down box select **'ZipCode'** *(should be inserted after ST and two spaces)*

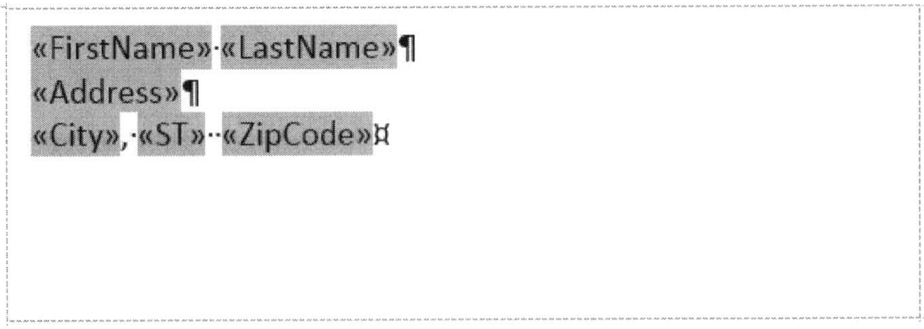

26. Click **'Next: Arrange your labels'**

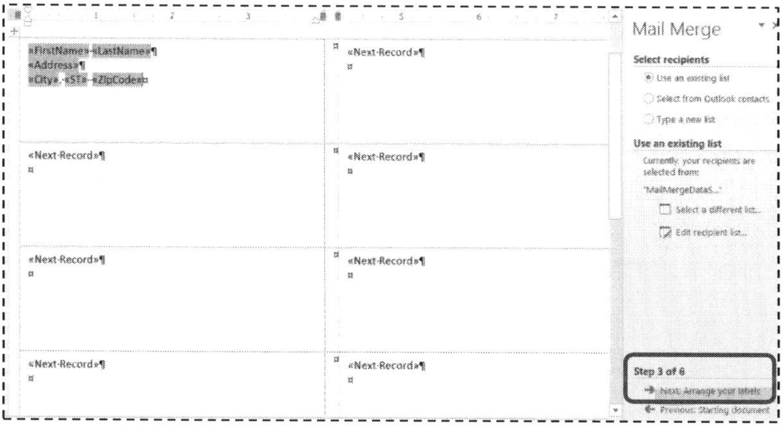

27. Under **'Replicate labels'** click the button **'Update all labels'**

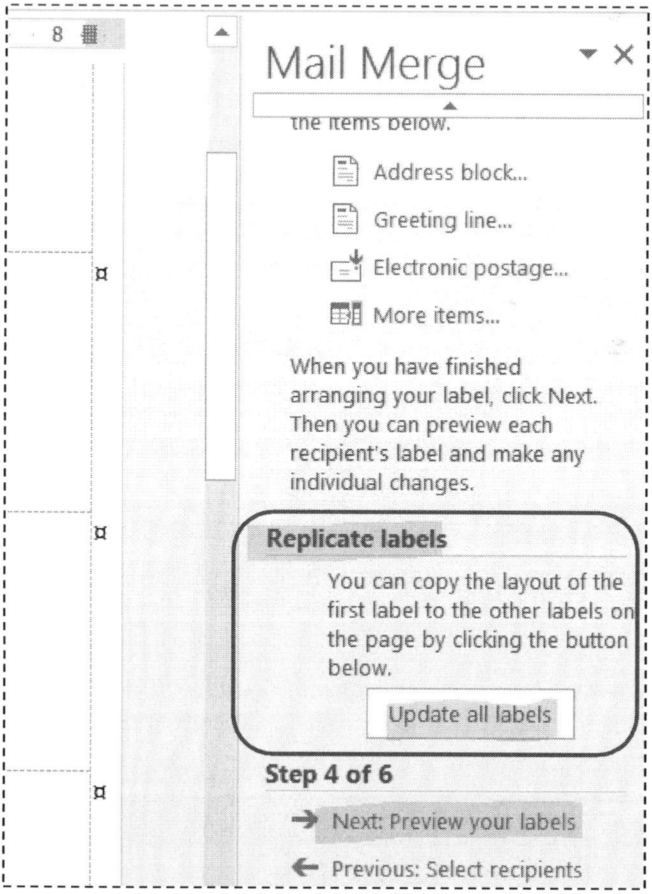

28. **Save** the labels to: **C:\MailMergeTraining**
29. Name the labels: **'Labels.docx'**

The SQL Prompt (opening a document containing merged fields)

After saving and closing a label document that contains merged fields, and then re-opening the label file, you're *linking* to a data source, Microsoft® refers to this as "database." As such, when opening a label file that contains merged fields you'll receive the following prompt, simply **click 'Yes'**, to proceed with opening the labels.

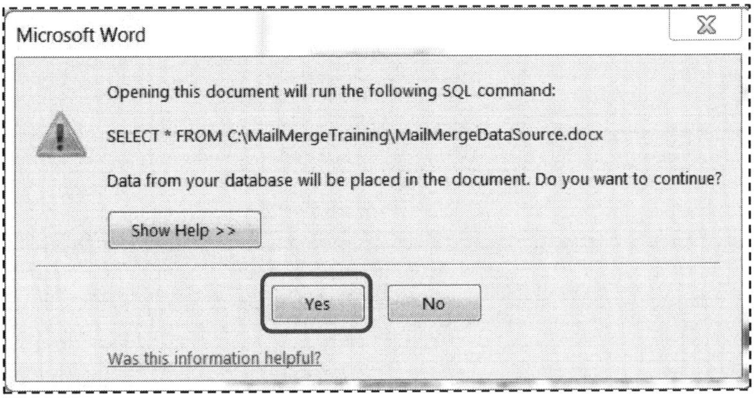

Merging The Labels

1. With the **'Labels'** document open, select the **'MAILINGS'** tab
2. Select the **'Finish & Merge'** drop-down box and then **'Edit Individual Documents…'**

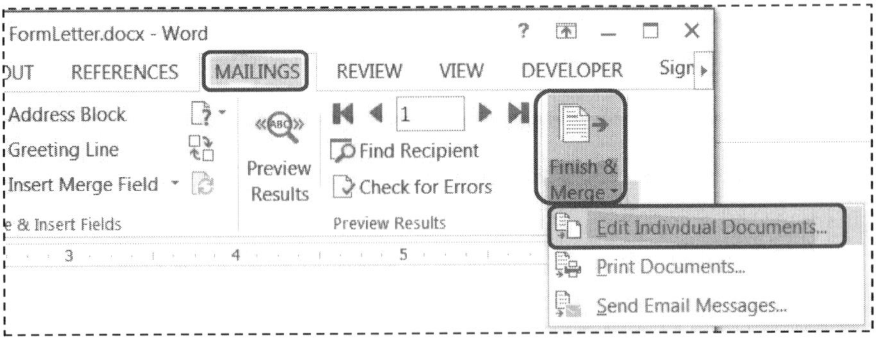

The following prompt should appear:

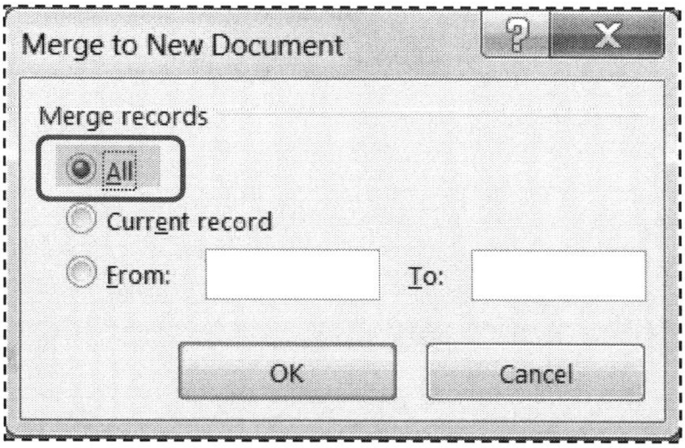

3. If not already selected, select the **'All'** radio button
4. Click the **'OK'** button

A new label document should now be created. Review the labels, if the results are as you expected them to be, you may *rename and save* the file or *print out* the labels for mailing.

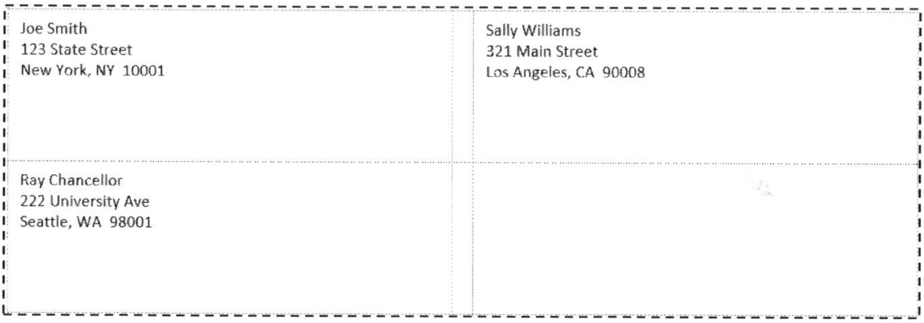

Appendix - A

Microsoft® Word® Shortcuts

The following lists some of the most common Microsoft® Word® shortcuts:

DESCRIPTION	COMMANDS
	FORMATTING
CTRL+B	Applies or removes **bold** formatting
CTRL+I	Applies or removes *italic* formatting
CTRL+U	Applies or removes underlining formatting
	FUNCTION
CTRL+A	Selects (highlights) the entire document
CTRL+C	Copies the contents of selected (highlighted) text
CTRL+X	Cuts the selected (highlighted) text
CTRL+V	Pastes the selected (highlighted) text, including all formatting
CTRL+F	Displays the Find and Replace dialog box, with the **Find** tab selected
CTRL+G	Displays the Find and Replace dialog box, with the **Go To** tab selected
CTRL+H	Displays the Find and Replace dialog box, with the **Replace** tab selected
CTRL+K	Displays the Insert Hyperlink dialog box for new hyperlinks or the Edit Hyperlink dialog box for selected existing hyperlinks
CTRL+N	Creates a new blank document
CTRL+O	Displays the dialog box to open a file
CTRL+S	Saves the active document with its current file name, location, and file format
CTRL+P	Displays the Print dialog box
CTRL+Z	The undo function will reverse the last command or delete the last entry you typed
	EDITING
F7	Runs Spellcheck
Shift + F7	Opens the Thesaurus dialogue box

A Message From The Author

Thank you for purchasing and reading this book! Your feedback is valued and appreciated! Please take a few minutes and leave a review.

Other Books Available From This Author:

---

1. Microsoft® Excel® Start Here The Beginners Guide
2. The Step-By-Step Guide To The **25 Most Common** Microsoft® Excel® Formulas & Features
3. The Step-By-Step Guide To **Pivot Tables &** Introduction To **Dashboards** *(version 2013)*
4. **Excel® Pivot Tables & Introduction To Dashboards** The Step-By-Step Guide *(version 2016)*
5. The Step-By-Step Guide To The **VLOOKUP** formula in Microsoft® Excel®
6. The Microsoft® Excel® Step-By-Step Training Guide **Book Bundle**
7. **Excel® Macros & VBA For Business Users** - A Beginners Guide

21046125R00063

Printed in Great Britain
by Amazon